The Eucharist's Biographer

The Eucharist's Biographer

The Liturgical Formation of Christian Identity

ALBERT J. D. WALSH

PICKWICK *Publications* · Eugene, Oregon

THE EUCHARIST'S BIOGRAPHER
The Liturgical Formation of Christian Identity

Pickwick Publications
An Imprint of Wipf and Stock Publishers
199 W. 8th Ave., Suite 3
Eugene, OR 97401

www.wipfandstock.com

ISBN 13: 978-1-61097-721-0

Cataloguing-in-Publication data:

Walsh, Albert J. D.

The eucharist's biographer : the liturgical formation of Christian identity / Albert J. D. Walsh.

xiv + 126 pp. ; 23 cm. Includes bibliographical references.

ISBN 13: 978-1-61097-721-0

1. Litugics. 2. Public worship. 3. I. Title.

BV176.3 .W357 2012

Manufactured in the U.S.A.

For the Lord of the Feast

Soli Deo Gloria

"I had always felt life first as a story:
and if there is a story there is a story-teller."
—G. K. CHESTERTON

With fond affection this work is dedicated to:
The Rev. Dr. Drake Williams of Tyndale Theological Seminary,
his wife Andrea, and their children, Henry, Abigail, and Samuel.
For their faith and service to Christ and the Church catholic,
their ecumenical spirit of grace, and their
example of genuine eucharistic joy.

Contents

Preface

THE TITLE FOR THIS essay is taken from the closing line of a poem titled "Transubstantiation" by Francis Thompson:

Man's body was ordained to tell
The tale of this sweet miracle.
For bread and wine, and all his food,
Are turned to Flesh, are turned to Blood;
And all men, at their common feasts,
Are transubstantiating priests.

Christ, as in Cana's miracle,
Generous, his creatures would excel,
So gave to men ordained the power
With his own Flesh and Blood to dower
The altar Bread, the altar Wine—
O daring plagiary divine!

Then walk awarely mid the corn
That will as human flesh be worn—
'Tis holy ground that thou dost tread.
And be indeed a worshipper,
Discerning in our daily bread
The Eucharist's biographer.[1]

I have not researched any one scholar's estimate of what, exactly, Francis Thompson proposed with that pregnant phrase of the last line in his poem, but I wonder if it is intended to reference the One who is Host at every *eucharistic-evangel*—that is, the Christ of God.[2] In any case, that is how I

---

1. Quoted in O'Connor, *Hidden Manna*, 35.

2. In using the neologism (i.e., eucharistic-evangel), I intend to reference that worshipful event that embodies both the *protestant-proclamatory principle* with its focus on the *Word* (as "spoken"), which is central to many if not most forms of traditional Protestant worship, and the *catholic-sacramental principle* with its focus on the *Word* (as "visible"), central to Roman Catholic/Pan-Orthodox liturgical practices; an embodiment

have chosen to read and interpret this line; the "biographer" is the One who has written and continues to write a *distinctive identity* in three uniquely and intimately related narrative forms: the eucharistic presence (i.e., what is often called the "real presence") in both forms as *Word* and *Sacrament*,[3] the Church (i.e., the body of Christ), and the individual believer (i.e., the member of the body with his or her exclusivity of being as well as character). As one who believes strongly in the ecumenical ministry and the need for renewal of its vision of greater visible unity; as one who has over the years grown increasingly dissatisfied with the "practice" of Holy Communion in the local congregation; as one who finds it increasingly difficult to defend (as in *apologetics*) the theology of this particular sacrament *strictly* from the perspective of Reformed faith (with the notable exception of the Mercersburg theology!)[4]; as one who wonders how we will ever recapture the genuine beauty and mystery of this glorious sacrament—I needed to research and write this essay for the benefit of the people of God I have been called to serve as an ordained minister in the United Church of Christ, to awaken renewed interest in the pursuit of greater visible unity, and in order

---

in which the two *principle* components are united in one inseparable liturgical event to be celebrated each and every Lord's Day.

3. In one of his closing chapters, George Hunsinger writes this in relation to the necessity of Word and Sacrament: "It is Christ who creates the community through Word and Sacrament. And he does so primarily through the Word, since the Word is prior to, embedded in, and more extensive than the Sacrament, though by the same token it might also be said that the Sacrament is more intensive, more graphic, and more corroborative than the Word. The primacy of the Word is such that it is efficacious apart from the Sacrament in a way that the Sacrament, for all its density, is not efficacious apart from the Word. The Word is fulfilled by the Sacrament, while the Sacrament is elucidated by the Word. Yet strictly speaking, it is only the Word, not the Sacrament, which is absolutely necessary for salvation. Normally, however, the two are mutually reinforcing and mutually interdependent, so that either would suffer without the other." *Eucharist and Ecumenism*, 261–62. With his use of the phrase "either would suffer without the other," Dr. Hunsinger touches directly on the theme of this essay and the fundamental import I place on the mutuality of *Word* and *Sacrament* as essential for the fullness of Christian liturgical expression on the Lord's Day.

4. In the preface to his monumental work of eucharistic theology, John Williamson Nevin wrote: "As the Eucharist forms the very heart of the whole Christian worship, so it is clear that the entire question of the church, which all are compelled to acknowledge—the great life problem of the age—centers ultimately in the sacramental question as its inmost heart and core. Our view of the Lord's Supper must ever condition and rule in the end our view of Christ's person and the conception we form of the church. It must influence, at the same time, very materially, our whole system of theology, as well as our ideas of ecclesiastical history." *Mystical Presence*, 23.

to remain faithful to my own ecumenical soul![5] This essay follows on the heels of my previously published work[6] and in some ways can be seen as a development of the argument made in that work of ecumenical theology. The eucharistic-evangel is the central liturgical event[7] in the life of the Church; some might say that it *is* the life of the Church—and I would be the first to affirm that assessment.

But if experience is a qualified teacher, I have learned that this sacrament has now become but another casualty in an embattled Church in which any semblance of ecumenical spirit has long since vanished from both pew and pulpit—and, regrettably, from the altar table as well. Moreover, there has evolved a related and rather peculiar phenomenon; many members of the local church will argue that because this sacrament is so very "special" it is best that it be celebrated *infrequently* or it will (as I have been informed on numerous occasions) "lose its meaning." What that "meaning" is, exactly, is terribly difficult to determine or define! I would suggest that this places the sacrament in the arena of "magic" rather than "mystery," and amounts to treating the Eucharist as if it were something akin to a family gathering on a holiday, an event reserved because it is "special"; its merit is in the "magic" it bestows in the glow of familial bonding around a common table, laden with all good food.[8]

5. The renowned Barthian scholar George Hunsinger has written, from the perspective of a Reformed theologian, what I consider to be one of *the* finest essays on the Eucharist and the ecumenical desire to achieve greater visible unity; what Dr. Hunsinger has achieved in this remarkable piece of ecumenical theology is unmatched in clarity of analysis, honesty of assessment, and fairness of proposal(s) for moving the ecumenical conversations beyond the current *impasse* regarding the Eucharist. This work has been an inspiration to much of my own proposal and deserves a wide readership, particularly among those who are invested in the ecumenical effort. See *Eucharist and Ecumenism*.

6. *United and Uniting: An Ecumenical Ecclesiology for a Church in Crisis.*

7. My use of *event* in relation to the eucharistic-evangel is intended to stress the unique character of this liturgical practice—one to be associated more with the drama of redemption than with a connected series of worshipful and fixed liturgical components. The use of this term implies movement, exchange, and interaction. While not wanting to risk an oversimplification of what I intend with the use of *event*, I would contend that the eucharistic-evangel embodies elements of drama not unlike those found in the realm of art and theatre, and cannot be appreciated for its depth by those who are merely "audience" to this event and not "participants" in both the unfolding drama and the degree to which it summons one to a transformed worldview as indicative of the very best in dramatic form.

8. One can readily see the poverty of such a perspective when held in contrast to the following affirmation: "Our blessed Saviour Jesus Christ instituted the Holy Communion of his Body and Blood, that it might be the abiding memorial of his atoning death; the

Call it hyperbole, but I have found few congregants who view this sacrament with the appropriate reverence it is due, and with a clear comprehension of how "mystery" resides at its core as a liturgical event. There is also a notable drought of appreciation for the way in which the eucharistic-evangel has been essential to what distinguishes Christian worship from all other forms of liturgical practice.[9] I cannot deny that in some respects this essay will appear far more polemic than did my first work of ecumenical theology, but that is not my intent. Rather, I am recommending a eucharistic theology that embodies the very best of the Great Tradition, manifests the spirit of *semper reformanda*, while seeking to advance the ecumenical effort toward greater visible unity.[10]

---

seal of his perpetual presence in the Church through the Holy Spirit; the mystical representation of the sacrifice of himself on the cross; the pledge of his undying love for his people; and the bond of his living union and fellowship with them to the end of time." Evangelical and Reformed Church, *Hymnal*, 32.

9. As a generalization Protestant traditions have tended to elevate the proclaimed *Word* as the essential characteristic of Christian worship, whereas the Roman Catholic, Orthodox, and other highly sacramental traditions have tended to elevate the *Sacrament* as the essential characteristic of Christian worship. As George Hunsinger has noted: "certain one-sidedness can be discerned in both the Reformed and Roman Catholic traditions. Historically, the predominant categories for the Reformed have been Word, witness, and teaching. The eucharist has been seen in this context, and the reality of mediation has been left to some extent in the shadows. For the Catholic tradition, the situation is much the reverse. Sacrament, mediation, and representation have been in the foreground. Preaching has been de-emphasized, and the reality of witness has been relegated to some extent to the margins." Hunsinger, *The Eucharist and Ecumenism*, 214. I would contend that this tendency can be addressed by a kind of *liturgical hypostasis* as the mirror image of the real and historical *hypostatic union* in Christ Jesus (the union of divine and human natures in one person). Understood in this fashion, the *Word* is that transcendent reality and real presence which is translated and disclosed through earthly realities (i.e., human words, language), while the *Sacrament* is those earthly realities (i.e., bread and wine) which are translated and disclosed as Real Presence and as transcendent reality. Because the hypostatic union is essential to the unity of Christ's person it is equally essential to his identity as Christ, Lord, Son of Man and Son of God; and because *this* is true Christ's identity in the liturgical matrix must correspond to that same reality evident in his identity as a historical person, divine and human.

10. George Hunsinger offers "seven guidelines" intended to inform the character and content of any ecumenical theology in its "special vocation." I have attempted throughout the body of this essay to bear these same guidelines in mind and not violate their implied integrity. Inclusively the seven are: (1) "Church-dividing views should be abandoned, especially in the form of false contrasts"; (2) "No tradition, including one's own, should be asked to compromise on essentials"; (3) "Where possible, misunderstandings from the past should be identified and eliminated"; (4) "Real differences should not be glossed over by resorting to ambiguity; they will come back to haunt theology and church"; (5)

During one session of our Bible study on a Sunday morning in which we were discussing the sacramental significance of the sixth chapter of John's Gospel, one of the participants asked why it was that we celebrated Holy Communion no more than eight times each year. Someone said in reply, "Because we truly reverence Communion, unlike the Catholics who seem to think it's a free ticket to heaven!" While I see no need to quibble over the obvious unawareness and complete absurdity of the comment, I do believe it reflects a general and commonly held misconception among many in the local congregation, one I hope to address if not rectify in this essay. Though my primary objective is to argue for the reinforcement of what I call a distinctive identity of the Christian, a secondary and related interest is with the establishment of a basis for advancing ecumenical conversations related to shared communion with brothers and sisters of other confessional and Christian bodies, while recognizing and acknowledging that such ecumenical dialogue involves sacramental issues of a theologically technical nature that are well beyond the scope of this essay and present expertise of this author.

In words that far excel any I could compose and yet resonate so clearly with the ecumenical intent of this essay, the renowned Church theologian of the last century, Karl Barth, wrote:

> The plurality of churches . . . should not be interpreted as something willed by God, as a normal unfolding of the wealth of grace given to [humankind] in Jesus Christ [nor as] a necessary trait of the visible, empirical Church, in contrast to the invisible, ideal, essential Church. Such a distinction is entirely foreign to the New Testament because, in this regard also, the Church of Jesus Christ is one. It is invisible in terms of the grace of the Word of God and of the Holy Spirit . . . but visible in signs in the multitude of those who profess their adherence to her; she is visible as a community and in her community ministry, visible in her service of word and sacrament. . . .[11]

"The range of acceptable diversity should be expanded as fully as possible within the bounds of fundamental unity"; (6) "All steps toward visible unity should be taken which can be taken without theological compromise"; and (7) "No one church should be expected to capitulate to another or be swallowed up into it." Hunsinger, *Eucharist and Ecumenism*, 9–10.

11. Quoted in Hunsinger, *Eucharist and Ecumenism*, 18.

Introduction

ORD AND SACRAMENT TOGETHER[1] form the essential and most influential liturgical matrix for the transformation and maintenance
of a distinctive Christian identity; this is the sum and substance of my
contention in this essay. I argue that the eucharistic-evangel, as a "means
of grace" and as the worship experience in which the "real presence"[2] of

---

1. Other than the use of a neologistic phrase, I make no claim to originality of
thought in this essay; within the glorious historical traditions of theological exposition
it would be a remarkable feat to actually provide *pure* originality, and besides, such is
not the most commendable aspect of any theological reflection. In fact, I deem it far
more important that I demonstrate how my proposal aligns in many respects with the
confessional communities to which I am indebted. In relation to my proposal of the necessary union of *Word* and *Sacrament* as vital to an essential and fuller liturgical matrix,
I appreciate the observations of George Hunsinger in his discussion of the eucharistic
theologies of both Luther and Calvin, when he writes: "The efficacy of the eucharist, according to Luther, was no different from that of the Word, because the content imparted
by both was identical. For Luther the eucharist was a particular form of God's Word, not
something independent of or alongside it. 'The same thing is present in the sermon,' he
stated, 'as in the sacrament' (*LW* 36, p. 348). As a visible form of the Word, the eucharist
testified concretely that Christ came also for the communicant in particular (*pro me*)."
And in reference to Calvin, he writes: "like Luther, Calvin believed that the content of
the gospel and that of the eucharist were the same—the living Christ himself—differing
only in their forms of presentation and reception, and therefore, to some extent, in their
function. Roughly speaking, while the gospel's function was to awaken faith and instruct
it, the eucharist was designed to nourish faith and renew it. The eucharist had to be seen,
Calvin believed, within the larger context of the gospel. That meant within the context of
our union with Christ, or *participatio Christi*, as established by the Holy Spirit through
faith." Hunsinger, *Eucharist and Ecumenism*, 33, 36.

2. "This real presence of His body and blood is the presence of Christ crucified and
glorified, here and now, under concrete signs. The meaning of every corporal presence is
to attest concretely the presence of that person that he may enter into a concrete communion. By the real presence of His body and blood, the Church knows that Christ is there
concretely in the midst and it receives Him by means of a concrete sign. The substantial
presence of Christ does not denote a material presence, in the natural sense, but the
presence of the profound reality of the body and blood of Christ crucified and glorified."
Thurian, *Eucharistic Memorial*, 2:121.

Jesus Christ is most clearly revealed, brings clarity to the identity of Jesus Christ as the crucified, risen, returning Lord, and that this revelation of Christ's particular identity and presence encounters, transforms, and maintains in grace the distinctive identity of the Christian. The unification of *Word* (as the *real presence* of Christ in the content of liturgical language in general and as Scripture read, interpreted, and proclaimed in particular; the *secondary* medium of God's self-communication)[3] and *Sacrament* (the *real presence* of Christ disclosed under the form of the consecrated and trans-elemented[4] bread and wine of the Eucharist; the *primary* medium of God's self-communication) enhances this transformative process.[5] The categorical terms of "secondary" and "primary" do not imply a *qualitative*

3. As is commonly known, Karl Barth spoke of the "Word of God" as Scripture, Jesus Christ, and Proclamation, respectively; the complexity of Barth's theological explication is well beyond the scope of this essay, but my use of the theological category of "Word" is intended, in the broadest sense, to resonate with this threefold form. The use of the rather awkward phraseology of "real presence/Real Presence" is not intended to imply the real presence of Christ in two separate yet equally important ways; rather I make this distinction in order to differentiate between the spiritual presence as "real" in the *Word* and the "Real" presence as disclosed in the *Sacrament*. I do not see how any further progress can be made in ecumenical dialogue as long as *either* one is underestimated as essential to Christ's presence in, with, and for his body, the Church in worship; and the fact that my entire thesis depends on the reunification of both *Word* and *Sacrament* demonstrates my desire to hold them together in a way that can only enrich the whole of the Christian worship!

4. See footnote 18 below for a full explication of this eucharistic category.

5. In his book *Corpus Mysticum*, Henri Cardinal de Lubac, in speaking of the *mystical* relationship between the Eucharist and the Church, offers the following quotation from another: ". . . That one body, which we many are, through the life-giving power of the Holy Spirit, is designated mystically by this sacrament, and it was clearly expressed in these words by the Apostle. In the Eucharist . . . the body of Christ, which is the Church . . . is intimated mystically, or sacramentally" (101). And in another work, F. W. Dillistone offers the following comment: "Within the Christian setting the Church is either the earthly symbolization of that universal structure within which the mutual self-offering of the eternal Godhead is forever being enacted or it is the earthly sign to mark off the place where the Divine presence is manifested and the Divine *opus* is performed. . . . Within the Christian context the first emphasis calls for a setting where the worshippers can gather together *around the Lord's table* and there renew the covenant with Him and with one another; the second emphasis calls for a setting where as many as possible can *hear* the testimony of what God has done in Christ and can respond by dedicating their wills to His service." Dillistone, *Christianity and Symbolism*, 70. In the former (de Lubac), there is a clear connection between the celebration of the Eucharist and the identity of the church as *Church* (i.e., "body of Christ"), while in the second observation (Dillistone) there is the implied reciprocated-duality of *Word* and *Sacrament* as equally essential to the identity of the Christian community (at worship and in life).

distinction between the two forms of Christ's real presence in the whole of the eucharistic-evangel; rather they are intended to assert Christ's true presence in two related yet substantially distinctive forms (again, not unlike, but perhaps more a mirror image of, the *hypostatic union* of traditional christological explication).

This particular characteristic of Christian worship, that is, the indispensable union of *Word* and *Sacrament* is distinctive to the Christian liturgical event of the eucharistic-evangel and therefore contributes sacramentally to the distinctive identity of the Christian in an inimitable manner.[6] For all of these stated reasons, and as evidence of her desire to be transformed as an aspect of being conformed to the image of Christ (individually and corporately), I also contend that all Protestant confessions and representative congregations, in the spirit of ecumenicity, give serious and theologically thoughtful consideration to a weekly celebration of the *Sacrament* in combination with the *Word*.[7]

6. "Under the new covenant Word and Sacrament are also equally united. Communion with God implies obedience to His Word as well as the reception of the body and blood of Christ. Christian worship also unites Word and Sacrament as two parts of one whole: the ministry of the Word and the ministry of the Sacrament." Thurian, *Eucharistic Memorial*, 2:54–55.

7. First, it is through the *Word* (as Scripture, preaching, responsive reading, prayers, liturgical format and content, and hymnic response) that God makes himself present (analogically/symbolically/spiritually) to/for the gathered community and individual worshipper. When the utterance of God is graciously given in and through human words—this is what I refer to throughout this essay as the "Word of God." The nature of human words is such that they have the potential to become the "Word of God"—the divine, illuminating "Logos." The christological significance of the term "Logos" bears decisively on my contention and proposal. Therefore, the *Sacrament* is to be comprehended and conditioned by words/the *Word*. I am fully aware of the necessity to maintain a clear and appropriate differentiation of the persons of the Trinity, and am equally conscious throughout this essay of the way in which the Church catholic has referenced the second person of the Trinity (namely, the Son) as the focal point of the theologically freighted term "Word." However, I would also want to emphasize the essential unity of Father and Son (bound as intimately as they are by the Love of the Holy Spirit) in order to avoid any impression that I have differentiated between the Father, Son, and Spirit so as to advance a form of tritheism or modalism. In short: Where the Father is, the Son is, the Holy Spirit is; where the Father is engaged, the Son is engaged, the Holy Spirit is engaged; what the Father honors, the Son honors, the Holy Spirit honors. While the "Word" is primarily the theological reference to the Son as the second person of the Trinity, the reserved nature of the title needs to be qualified. It is not intended to do so in such a way that the Son is to be isolated in any way from the Father and Holy Spirit; nor would we want to suggest that the Father and Holy Spirit have been vacated from any activity associated with the Son as "Word."

Those familiar with the arguments that seek to support and legitimate the weekly celebration of the Eucharist know that such cases made are multifaceted and in some cases extremely complex. For example, while some argue that such practice has warrant in the traditions of the nascent or ancient Christian church, others contend that such was also the practice of the Reformation churches, or at least the recommended practice for traditions stemming from Luther and Calvin. Both these and other contentions have merit; nevertheless I have chosen to focus attention on the unity of *Word* and *Sacrament* as essential to the transformation and maintenance of a distinctive Christian identity, and therefore to be celebrated on a weekly basis. I am not so much arguing for an identity that lends itself to the pride of "exclusivity," as there is already far too much evidence of such in the present structures of denominational pride. I am interested in advancing a form of Christian identity that is distinctive in the sense that it shapes the whole of both individual and communal realities to such a degree that it becomes evident in a worldview that is contrary to the prevailing ideology of contemporary (postmodern) culture.[8]

In his insightful book *Visible Unity and Tradition*, Max Thurian writes: "God is the living actualization of the perfect unity of three persons—the Father, the Son, and the Holy Spirit. As unity and trinity he is the pattern of all unity in heaven and on earth, and of the unity of the Church above all. For the three persons act in perfect harmony, in accordance with one common will and in full unity, yet the Father being only Father, the Son only the Son, and the Holy Spirit only the Holy Spirit. In this way the members of the Body of Christ, the Church, must in all their multiplicity and their entire individual distinctness one from another, tend towards that perfect harmony, that shared will, that full unity, which they contemplate in the Trinity" (3).

8. By use of the term "identity" I intend more than the common identifications (e.g., one's family of origin, homeland, profession or occupation, name, marital status, etc.) we tend to associate with it. I am referencing the deeper dynamic of "who" one is *essentially* and the "telos" of one's being and life *as a whole*. My assumption is that we have been created for specificity and essentially for communion with God, so that our "identity" has a transcendent dimension, often ignored or overlooked, and sometimes undervalued. I associate "identity" with that now classic phrase from the *Confessions* of St. Augustine: "Man is one of your creatures, Lord, and his instinct is to praise you . . . since he is part of your creation, he wishes to praise you. The thought of you stirs him so deeply he cannot be content unless he praises you, because you have made us for yourself and our hearts find no peace until they rest in you" (*Confessions*, Bk. 1, 21). I would contend that there continues to be a sense in which the "hearts (of our contemporaries) find no peace"—and will find no peace until they discover the fulfillment of their true identity as children of God, transformed and re-created in the image of Christ Jesus. Stated in the broadest of terms, I perceive that identity (as I intend the term) "can be explained by the fact of our resemblance to Christ and our absolute and manifold dependence upon Him. The Lord is the model of all our virtues, the principle of all our hopes, the expiation of all our sins,

Moreover, I would affirm that the eucharistic-evangel (as union of *Word* and *Sacrament*) constitutes the central event of all Christian worship, as the heart and soul of all liturgical celebrations. In addition I would argue that the worship of the Christian community is severely truncated in the absence of a weekly celebration of the Eucharist; this sacramental act cannot be considered optional, as though it was at the discretion of church leaders—even the pastor—to determine when and if the Eucharist is to be celebrated. While obligatory language may seem to some far too heavy-handed, I suggest that the effects of infrequent celebration of the Eucharist in most Protestant churches has been detrimental to the development and maintenance of a distinctive Christian identity among those whose very lives have been marked (in baptism) by the crucified and risen Christ whose "real presence" is superlatively disclosed in the eucharistic-evangel.[9]

There can be little doubt that we live in an historical period wherein the identity of the Christian is being seriously challenged from several quarters; for example, the demands of spiritualistic relativism and the impact the "seeker" movement have had on worship practices throughout the church, the philosophical perspectives of secularism, a growing right wing movement in Christian communities which defines the identity of the Christian life in terms of a narrowly designated moral obligation, a deepening sense of frustration and desperation concerning the fate of the

the source of all our supernatural life. He is the exemplary and meritorious cause of our justification, and in a certain sense even its final and efficient cause. He is our Emmanuel, our Master, our guide, our friend, our brother; in fine, He is our all, and before God we are nothing except with Him and through Him. In a word, we are joined to Him by all the bonds that attach one man to another; and here these bonds are far more numerous and far more powerful." Mersch, *The Whole Christ*, 9–10. Biblical scholar Udo Schnelle offers the following: "The forming of identity always occurs under the influence of one or more cultural contexts. Thus one's sense of identity in belonging to a particular ethnic group is essentially determined by objectifiable characteristics such as language, genealogy, religion, and the traditions that have developed within the group. Traditions, in turn, reflect cultural molding through texts, rituals, and symbols. Although, as a rule, identity-formation occurs within such a context, it always has a process character, if fluid, and is bound to changing situations." Schnelle, *Theology of the New Testament*, 55.

9. Dom Cyprian Vagaggini, OSB, provides the following concept of the liturgy of the church: "The liturgy is the complexus of the sensible signs of things sacred, spiritual, invisible, instituted by Christ or by the Church; signs which are efficacious, each in its own way, of that which they signify; by which signs God (the Father by appropriation), through Christ the Head and Priest, and in the presence of the Holy Spirit, sanctifies the Church, and the Church as a body, in the presence of the Holy Spirit, uniting herself to Christ her Head and Priest, through Him renders her worship to God (the Father by appropriation)." Vagaggini, *Theological Dimensions of the Liturgy*, 25.

earth and the human community coupled with a growing cynicism and pessimism, a shrinking planet which has brought about a previously unparalleled exposure to a plurality of religious traditions, perspectives, and patterns of belief, an emerging class of young adults unable to grasp any genuine hope for the future, focusing instead in the present as the medium of personal if not self-involved enrichment, delineated for the most part in terms of material gain and upward mobility.[10]

All these, and more, have played their part in frustrating, complicating, and aggravating the development, maturation, and maintenance of a distinctive Christian identity. At this point it would be helpful to say specifically what I mean when I refer to a distinctive Christian identity. As mentioned briefly above, I certainly do not mean to suggest any form of identity thought to be unique to any one confessional body of Christian believers over against all others, so that members of that particular community of faith can be set apart from all other Christian believers. That would be contrary to the intent of this essay in more ways than can be stated! When I use the term "distinctive," I intend its use as an adjective, a descriptive of a sacramental, *eucharistically shaped* differentiated identity, which can be seen in all of its particulars, as informed by and maintained within the context of the Christian tradition and worship *as a whole*; it is that personal and corporate identity shaped and conformed to the "image of Christ," which embraces the whole of a person so that his or her entire reality and worldview are impacted as well. Faith, of course, plays a central role in this process of assimilation or incorporation which has as its outcome the transformation of identity; and faith, in the broadest sense of the term, is more than mere assent to a set of doctrinal or dogmatic assertions. Faith itself is holistic and fundamentally relational, placing the recipient

10. Although his concern is with the issues surrounding the necessity for both clergy and laity to gain a deeper appreciation for and comprehension of what is commonly called "historical theology," Gregg Allison's general assessment of factors adversely affecting the spiritual health of the church in our contemporary setting is relevant. Allison writes, "A fourth benefit that historical theology renders the church is to *protect against the individualism that is rampant today* among Christians. Tragically, numerous forces—a consumerist mentality, an insistence on individual rights, an emphasis on personal autonomy, a pronounced sense of entitlement—have converged to foster an atmosphere in which too many Christians pick and choose their doctrines like they pick and choose their clothes or fast-food meals. . . . Thankfully, historical theology can act as a corrective to this regrettable situation. It reminds believers that theirs is a corporate faith. . . . This rich heritage protects against the tendency to select the doctrines one likes and to reject those one does not like, thus giving in to one's sinful propensities." Allison, *Historical Theology*, 26.

of such faith in a personal, intimate, and yet mediated relationship to the living God in and through Christ Jesus.[11]

11. Richard P. McBrien defines faith as "personal knowledge of God, and Christian faith as personal knowledge of God in Christ . . . it is clear that faith is indeed personal knowledge of God, but there is much more to it than that."

McBrien goes on to assert the dynamics of faith in a way that I find immensely helpful to my purposes in this essay. He enumerates the dimensions of a dynamic faith in the following characterizations:

"1. Although faith is personal knowledge of God, that knowledge is always achieved and activated within a given community of faith, whether the Church as we know it or some other religious body, and beyond that within the whole human family.

2. This knowledge of God is not merely knowledge in the cognitive or intellectual sense, although it *is* that too. It is a knowledge which implies trust and a total commitment of the self to God, a commitment of heart as well as of mind.

3. Faith is not just the knowledge of God in general, but the knowledge of God which comes through the reception and acceptance of God's word. In the Christian sense, faith is the acceptance of God's-Word-made-flesh in Jesus Christ, and then of the preaching of that Word by the Apostles and the Church.

4. The acceptance of God's word in Christ and in the Church demands not only intellectual assent but also obedience—obedience to the Commandments and to the New Law of the Gospel, which calls us to work for social and political liberation as well as personal transformation of the individual.

5. If there is to be genuine obedience, there must be some acknowledgement of past failures, a conversion (*metanoia*, or change of mind), and repentance.

6. Faith always remains free. The 'evidence' for faith is never overwhelming. There are signs and witnesses. But these are always external and never finally persuasive in themselves. The only motive of faith that ultimately counts is internal: the presence of the Holy Spirit.

7. On the other hand, faith and reason are not absolutely separate. Even if one does not 'reason to' faith, faith must always be 'consonant with reason.' Thus, St. Paul urges us to worship God 'in a way that is worthy of thinking beings' (Romans 12:1). . . .

8. Faith is a matter of the highest human importance, because without it we cannot be justified or saved. But since God wishes the salvation of all persons, faith must be available in principle even to those outside the Church." McBrien, *Catholicism*, 1:45–46.

We must not underestimate the importance and centrality of "faith" to the entire process of transformation and maintenance of the *distinctive* identity being proposed in this essay! Familiarity with the entire Pauline corpus demonstrates the centrality of "faith" to every aspect of the Christian life in Christ and to the conformation to Christ's "image" implicit in the relational characteristic of the Holy Spirit's presence and empowerment. One must also maintain the tension evident in the language of the epistle of James (2:14–26 in particular!) in which the author argues for the essential bond between "faith" and "works"; faith is demonstrable in both an *internal* transformation and an *external*

To be even more particular, it is that form of identity shaped by: (1) dying together with Christ (Rom 6:3; 2 Cor 6:9; Col 2:12); (2) that condition of life best expressed in the words of the Apostle Paul when he wrote, "It is no longer I who live, but Christ who lives in me" (Gal 2:20); (3) the life shared with the risen Lord in the Spirit (Rom 5–6; 2 Cor 5); (4) a form of life that continually grows and unfolds, becoming manifest as the glory of eternal life (Rom 5:17, 6: 5, 22; 2 Cor 2:16). This distinctive identity is one wholly governed by the life known in Christ and sustained by the Spirit (1 Cor 2:16, 7:40; Rom 8:26–27, 12:2). Furthermore, it is an identity shaped by love as the gift of the Spirit (1 Cor 12:31—13:1), the objects of such love being God (Rom 8:28), the neighbor (Rom 13:8–9), and the fellowship of believers (Rom 12:20; 1 Thess 4:9). Finally, the virtues of such an identity and form of life are the harvest of the Spirit in cooperation with the Lord (Phil 2:12f.; Gal 5:22; 1 Cor 4:21; 2 Cor 3:17–18). In the strict sense, this distinctive identity is one conformed to the identity of Christ, as a form-of-life constituted by and expressed in love, obedience to the Father, forgiveness, mercy, patience, and hope.

Although the Christian cannot separate him or herself from the cultural and social milieu of existence, the nature of the dilemma I am addressing raises the pertinent question: Among the multiplicity of influences which can determine the molding of a distinctive Christian identity, which can be said to be central, critical, and crucial to the transformation and maintenance of such an identity? There is a derivative question of equal, if not surpassing, importance: If there should be such a central, critical, and crucial influence upon the transformation and maintenance of a distinctive Christian identity, is such an influence locatable within the more catholic and ecumenical patterns of the Christian tradition? Is there a unifying principle, of *ecumenical* proportion(s), which can bind all forms of Christian identity together, that is, a catholic principle underlying a distinctive Christian identity?

My purpose in this essay is to demonstrate the viability of such an influential principle, locatable within the generous and catholic patterns of Christian liturgical tradition, contributing to its *ecumenical* scope. The unparalleled unification of *Word* and *Sacrament* is that form of worship expression that qualifies as a distinctively Christian liturgical expression, which is also the central, critical, and crucial influence in the transformation

---

and relational adjustment to a lifestyle disclosing the transformation of identity in Christ and under the direction of the Spirit.

and maintenance of a distinctive Christian identity. It is this factor that makes the argument for the *weekly* celebration of the Eucharist as sacrament, in combination with the present practice of focusing on Scripture and Proclamation, fundamentally important to both the Church as the "body of Christ" and the individual believer as a member of Christ's body.[12]

While I would acknowledge the impact of a solid and comprehensive ministry of Christian education on the transformation and maintenance of Christian identity, my interest is more intentionally to explore the liturgical life of the Christian community and the influence participation in the liturgy of eucharistic-evangel (as unification of *Word* and *Sacrament*) has in the formation and maintenance of a distinctive Christian identity. Such interest has come after thirty years of service to the local congregation as an ordained minister of the United Church of Christ, and with the developing recognition that for many, if not most, members of the local congregation, Sunday worship is the singular point of exposure to the traditions and theology of the Christian faith. I have also become increasingly concerned to see Christian identity defined in some of the most bizarre and restrictive ways, through characterizations that have absolutely nothing to do with the traditions of the faith and far more to do with current fashions in cultural fascinations with something glibly called "new age spirituality." For example, it is not uncommon to hear contemporary Christians define one aspect of their spiritual character as having more to do with the religious concept of reincarnation than resurrection![13]

12. "One of the dynamic elements of contemporary liturgical thought and practice is a re-embracing of the twofold liturgy suggested by Luke 24—their 'hearts burned within them' as Christ opened the Word, and they recognized the risen Christ 'in the breaking of the bread.' The Roman Catholic Church has with Vatican II consistently sought to restore the liturgy of the Word to its rightful place within Christian worship: there is no proper celebration of the Lord's Supper without the proclamation of the Word in some form or another. And many on the Protestant and evangelical side have grown in their conviction that the preached Word is necessarily complemented by the ministry of the Table. Noteworthy here is the conviction that the Word comes prior, and that the Word is received and embodied through the celebration of the Lord's Supper." "Lord's Supper," in Dyrness and Kärkkäinen, eds., *Global Dictionary of Theology*, 508.

13. "A growing number of Westerners prefer to identify themselves as 'spiritual' rather than as 'religious.' It has been suggested that even about half of the European Union citizens could be defined as 'believing but not belonging' (Introvigne). Their belief system holds a concept of God that does not necessarily resemble that of historical Christianity, preferring the pantheistic, immanent, subjectively experienced godhood within. Terms like 'spirituality,' 'holism,' 'New Age,' 'mind-body-spirit,' 'yoga,' 'energies,' 'feng shui,' 'guru,' 'ch'I,' 'rebirth,' 'karma' and 'chakra' are becoming more and more common in the

In the sacramental mode, that which distinguishes us as Christian disciples, across the wide spectrum of confessional, theological, and liturgical styles, is profoundly expressed by a saying commonly attributed to the Church Fathers, where an affirmation was offered during the distribution of the consecrated elements of the Eucharist to each communicant: "take and eat what you are!"[14] There can be little doubt that the Eucharist is the heart of the whole of Church in worship and being; the symbolic re-*presentation* of Christ is reinforced within the sacramental re-*enactment* of the identity of Christ Jesus in the whole of his resurrected and glorified existence as the One who still bears on his glorified body the marks of his passion! As disciples of *this* Christ, who offered his church in her nascent form (i.e., the twelve at table on that fateful night of his betrayal and arrest) a self-definition as *eucharistically* informed, we are called to an identity, in both its corporate and individual dynamics, that is a manifestation of his presence to and for the world—a presence that is fundamentally one

---

Western vocabulary. The bedside-table religiosity of the West is in transition and is less and less Christian today." "New Religious Movements, Christian," in Dyrness and Kärkkäinen, eds., *Global Dictionary of Theology*, 603–4.

14. "It is often stated in the tradition that it is our bodies and souls which are transformed by the substance of Christ's flesh, not the other way round." Hunsinger, *Eucharist and Ecumenism*, 64. The late Dr. T. F. Torrance once wrote of "the ecumenical perspective" brought about by "the convergence of two movements of thought: (*a*) the recovery of a high, non-dualist Christology, in which the focus of attention is on the humanity of the incarnate Son of God, i.e., upon *God as Man* rather than upon God in Man; and (*b*) the recovery of the eucharistic pattern of worship and life in which the primacy is given to the priestly mediation of Jesus Christ. Each inevitably affects and modifies the other, but the fruit of their convergence seems to be yielding a much profounder and more truly Catholic understanding of the Eucharist." Torrance, *Theology in Reconciliation*, 135. However, it is in what follows that I discover resonance with the kind of "transformation" implied in my own essay: "Behind the former movement of thought lies a rejection of every deistic disjunction between God and the world and the world and a fresh understanding of the mighty living God who interacts with the created world of space and time. Here we have a doctrine of God which combines the Patristic emphasis upon the Being of God in his Acts with the Reformed emphasis upon the Acts of God in his Being, leading to a doctrine of the incarnation of the Son or Word of God within the space and time of our creaturely world, in whose Person being and act are inseparably one, and in whom therefore all that he has done for us in his union with us in our historical and creaturely actuality remains a present hypostatic reality creating and inviting communion with us in the space-time structure of our existence. This leads to a profounder doctrine of the real presence of the whole Jesus Christ whose historical life and passion, far from being past, persist through the triumph of the resurrection over all corruption and decay as continuing living reality which Jesus Christ through the Holy Spirit mediates to us in our present space-time existence in the Eucharistic worship of the Church." Ibid.

of compassion with and for the suffering of humanity and the groaning of creation itself.

The fuller liturgical aspect, consisting of *Word* and *Sacrament,* is the worshipful environment *par excellence,* which assures the transformation and maintenance of a distinctive Christian identity, subject each "eighth day" to that grace which will assure the continued growth and enrichment of an identity unlike any other in this world, and yet one that is always and ever *for* the world, though never *of* the world! Implicit in the whole of what this essay embodies is the affirmation that the union of *Word* and *Sacrament* (as I have defined this liturgical reality) is the source from which the church will draw her life and the eschatological goal toward which she will live her life in faithful obedience to the unforgettable affirmation of the Apostle Paul, who wrote: "For as often as you eat this bread and drink the cup, you proclaim the Lord's death until he comes" (1 Cor 11:26).[15]

While I make use of the term "transformation" throughout this essay, I could just as well have made use of the term "transfiguration," and done so as the deeper meaning and intent of "transformation," captured in this significant term with even greater force.[16] In particular, I would note the phrase in the footnote below in which Tertullian writes, "for everything that is transfigured into something else ceases to be what it was and begins to be what it was not." Although the reference is not to the individual communicant, it can be said to apply to the church in the eucharistic-evangel

15. "In the Eucharist, which is to be placed within the context of the paschal meal and makes use of certain of its themes, the Church, according to the command of its Lord, performs an action 'for the memorial of Christ,' to give thanks for the unique and perfect act of deliverance through the passion and the resurrection, to give thanks also because this deliverance is actualized in the sacrament, to ask God that it may be applied to each man by the coming of Christ to him and in him and that the Messiah may come again soon to accomplish in splendor for the whole universe, in the Kingdom, what He has already accomplished in a hidden manner, in Himself, in the condescension of His incarnation. . . . Like the paschal meal, the Eucharist moves from faith in deliverance, which has been accomplished and is actualized in the sacrament, to a prayer that the Lord may come for every man and thus hasten the last day." Thurian, *Eucharistic Memorial,* 1:29.

16. As stated by James T. O'Connor, the term *transfiguration* "means that a thing ceases to be what it was and becomes what it was not. This is the sense already given to the word by Tertullian, who used it when speaking of the Incarnation. Tertullian had written: 'it must be asked how the Word became Flesh. Was he transfigured [*transfiguratus*] into Flesh, or did he put on Flesh? We have to say 'put on Flesh,' since it is necessary to believe that God is immutable . . . as well as eternal. Transfiguration [*transfiguration*] is the making an end of [*interemptio*] what was formerly there: for everything that is transfigured [*transfiguratur*] into something else ceases to be what it was and begins to be what it was not." O'Connor, *Hidden Manna,* 40.

(Augustine's "you are that which you receive"), as a symbol (*semenia*) of christological identification; I contend that the individual identity of each believer, as is true for the whole of the corporate body, is in actuality transformed or "transfigured" (proleptic change) in and through the sacrosanct empowerment of the *Word* and *Sacrament*.

The use of the parenthetical "proleptic change" in the last sentence is intended to draw attention to the manner in which care must be taken so that there is not even the implication that this identity transformation of the believer can reach perfection—in other words, the attainment of identity in and with Christ as an internalized reality, externally manifested, cannot (in this life) reach either fulfillment or completion (as in perfection). Such perfection awaits eschatological fulfillment in the return of Christ and in the kingdom of God. The narrative of Christ's "transfiguration" (Luke 9:28–36, parallels), in which Jesus Christ is witnessed in his "glory" by three of his disciples, suggests that this particular vision is proleptic in character and can serve as paradigmatic of the way in which the identity of the Christian believer, transformed/transfigured through the liturgical encounter with the "real presence" of Christ, is itself anticipatory in nature.[17]

The future and glorified Christ cannot be abstracted from the crucified and risen Christ, as is evidenced in the account of the same vision in Matthew's gospel (Matt 17:9–12!), where Jesus offers a clarification on his identity, post-transfiguration, in which suffering, death, and resurrection become as characteristic of his true identity as Messiah as is his future glorification. The believer cannot hope for the fulfilled attainment of identity in Christ in this life (we are and remain *simul justus et peccator*, righteous and at the same time a sinner), but can with all good faith embrace the promise of future perfection of identity in the proleptic reality of his or her sharing in/with the true identity of Christ in the present.[18] On just this point we also want to recall that superb phrase of the Apostle Paul: "For as often as you eat this bread and drink the cup, you proclaim the Lord's

---

17. "Because of Christ and of the oath sealed with His blood on the cross, the Church today can pray and wait in confidence for the promises of resurrections, present and future, accomplished by the Father in His Son. The Church is at one with Christ, the son of David, and waits with Him; she prays in Him and by Him for the resurrection, the return of the Messiah, the eternal Kingdom, and she can cry aloud in the liturgy of the Eucharist: *Maranatha*; Yes, come Lord Jesus (I Cor. 16:22; Rev. 22:20)." Thurian, *Eucharistic Memorial*, 1:31.

18. I am grateful to Ms. Carolyn Crouthamel for this insight into the proleptic character of "transfiguration" as related to identity configuration in Christ.

death until He comes" (1 Cor 1:26), where reference to the "Lord's death" is every bit as essential to Christ's true identity as is the reference to his future glorification ("until He comes").[19]

If as I among others would contend there is rampant in our contemporary setting an unhealthy obsession with the "individual," even in the church (e.g., individual rights, individual choice, individual emotional needs, etc.), then the eucharistic-evangel offers a profoundly important sacramental setting for the enrichment of individual identity as dependent upon corporate connections. In other words, the very nature of the eucharistic-evangel (*Word* and *Sacrament*) is one in which the *Sacrament* mitigates an otherwise obsessive preoccupation with the "individual" in isolation, in that one cannot define one's self in terms other than those one has received in, through, and by the corporate body of Christ, and one in which the *Word*, as the biblical-theological heritage, reinforces the corporate dimensions of a liturgical reality that has formed and maintained the individual aspect of Christian identity for centuries.[20]

Just as the Eucharist as *Sacrament* defines the body of Christ as the corporate reality, so the biblical-theological-liturgical language of the Church catholic as *Word* reinforces the unique character of the individual Christian as a member of that same body which is seen in the bread that is

19. "Because we are united to Christ who is bone of our bone and flesh of our flesh, and participate in the risen humanity of Jesus, eschatology is essential to our faith. Union with Christ means union with the Christ who rose again from the dead, who ascended to the right hand of the Father and who will come again; and therefore union with Christ here and now carries in its heart the outreach of faith toward the resurrection of the dead and the renewal of heaven and earth at the Second Advent of Christ. The crucial issue in Calvin's eschatology is *the humanity of the risen Christ*, and our actual participation in His humanity through Word and Sacrament." Torrance, *Conflict and Agreement in the Church*, 1:98.

20. "As the sole saving agent, Christ is always the central acting subject in both Word and Sacrament. Called into being by proclamation, and ruled by the authority of scripture, the church is a creature of God's Word (*creatura verbum dei*). Founded in baptism and nourished by the eucharist, the church is also a creature of the sacraments (*creatura sacramenti*). While the Word is the normative vehicle of Christ's self-witness, it is also the vehicle of his self-impartation to faith. In turn, while the sacraments are more nearly vehicles of his self-mediation, they are also vehicles of his self-witness at the same time. The eucharist uniquely manifests the downward and upward vectors of Christ's presence in his office as the Mediator, for it is both a vehicle of his self-impartation (*koinonia*) and most especially of his eternal self-offering on the basis of his finished work (intercession). Here and now, whether by Word or Sacrament, Christ always attests and mediates himself in the Spirit by way of self-anticipation as the firstfruits of his final return in glory (*arrabon/aparche*)." Hunsinger, *Eucharist and Ecumenism*, 184–85.

broken and the cup that is poured out.[21] A church enamored with culture and contemporary agendas will find it difficult to appreciate the importance of what is being affirmed; the eucharistic-evangel, as proposed in this essay, is a critical factor in that it poses a very real challenge to all forms of individualism *and* exclusivism, in the real presence of him who is both Lord and Christ, reminding the church that her true identity is concealed in the consecration and *transelementation*[22] of bread and wine, as it is in attentiveness to and internalization of the *Word*.

21. In language that is far more insightful and eloquent than is my own, Henri de Lubac expresses what I struggle to convey when he writes: "Now, the Eucharist is the mystical principle, permanently at work at the heart of the Christian society, which gives concrete form to this miracle. It is the universal bond; it is the ever-springing source of life. Nourished by the body and blood of the Saviour, his faithful people thus all 'drink of the one Spirit,' who truly makes them into a single body. Literally speaking, therefore, the Eucharist makes the church. It makes of it an inner reality. By its hidden power, the members of the body come to unite themselves by becoming more fully members of Christ, and their unity with one another is part and parcel of their unity with the one single Head. This unity of the head and of all the rest of the body, the unity of Christ and of his Church—*He is her head, she is his body*—is more than what is normally called 'the whole body of the Church' or even 'the body of Christ in general.' It constitutes a real being." De Lubac, *Corpus Mysticum*, 88–89.

22. Knowing full well that the use of this freighted theological term will cause some within my own confessional community to question whether, in fact, I remain "Reformed" in any meaningful sense of the term, and while acknowledging how this sacramental category is held most ardently by the Orthodox Churches, I nevertheless believe its use to be consonant with the ecumenical spirit in general, and the ecumenical characteristics of the United Church of Christ in particular. Embracing this primarily Eastern term as essential to our conceptual language of the Eucharist is, I believe, indicative of the genuine desire to move forward in visible unity, and representative of maturation in the development of a more robust sacramental theology. George Hunsinger writes: "Orthodoxy, which wishes to avoid being overly scholastic in its doctrinal formulations, permits a range of other possibilities, including the ancient patristic doctrine of 'transelementation" (*metastoicheiosis*). The substance of this idea, as it turns out, can also be found in Luther as well as in the Reformed theologians Vermigli, Cranmer, and Bucer. Adopting it would perhaps not require a great adjustment in the views of Calvin. Here is a largely forgotten idea which, if officially embraced by Protestant communities, could conceivably move them—at this momentous point—from a stance that was church-dividing to one within the bounds of acceptable diversity." Hunsinger, *Eucharist and Ecumenism*, 12. And tracing the patristic origins of the same term, James O'Connor observes: "The Word's assimilation of the Eucharistic elements to himself—as assimilation by which they become his Body and Blood—is described by the forceful Greek word *metastoikeiosas*, transelementation. It actually means a restructuring of the elements, since the Greek *stokeia* means 'fundamental elements or principles'. . . . Gregory (of Nyssa) also clearly teaches that this 'transelementation' occurs immediately at the Consecration, 'through the power of the blessing,' as he phrases it. The fact that this happens at the Consecration

While I respect that there will be those who undoubtedly have difficulty with my proposal that reclamation of the theological category of "transelementation" is timely and relevant to the development of a contemporary Protestant eucharistic theology, I would also contend that the use of this particular sacramental language and the theological realities it represents are critical to any attempt to move ecumenical conversations beyond the present impasse. As the Reformed theologian and Barthian scholar George Hunsinger, in his superlative piece of ecumenical theology, has written:

> The idea of transelementation, as represented by Vermigli, Bucer, and Cranmer (and based on patristic sources), would allow the Reformed churches to maintain their historic concern for Christ's bodily integrity while moving closer to the high sacramental traditions on real presence. It would mean a further step toward healing intolerable ecumenical divisions. Nothing essential would be lost for the Reformed, while something valuable would be gained. Nothing would be compromised, but something unexpected would be embraced. Finding a principled way to accept views which it had been previously thought necessary to reject is the soul of the ecumenical project.[23]

Those most familiar with the sixth chapter of the Gospel according to St. John are already aware that a sizable portion of that same chapter is devoted to the teaching of Jesus regarding the "eating" of his flesh and the "drinking" of his blood, and the controversy it created among some of the Jewish leaders and disciples of Jesus. One of the closing lines reads, "Therefore, when many of His disciples heard this, they said, 'This teaching

---

and not 'through our eating' indicates that it is not the faith of the believer that makes Christ present; his Presence is due to the power of the sanctification or Consecration (the same Greek word, *hagiazo*, can be translated as either of these), apart from the faith of the believer, as later theological reflection will make even clearer." O'Connor, *Hidden Manna*, 35–36.

    In his discussion of the term "transelementation" and in relation to its use in the eucharistic theology of the Reformed scholar Vermigli, George Hunsinger states that "the image which illustrated transelementation was that of an iron rod thrust into the fire. Just as the iron was transformed by its participation in the fire, so was the consecrated element transformed by its sacramental union with Christ's flesh. In and with this transforming union, the distinction between the two was maintained. Just as the iron did not cease to be iron, or the fire fire, so did the bread not cease to be bread, or Christ's flesh his flesh. In the mystery of their sacramental union they formed a unique distinction-in-unity and unity-in-distinction." Hunsinger, *Eucharist and Ecumenism*, 41.

    23. Ibid., 51–52.

is hard! Who can accept it?'" (John 6:60). Frankly, I would imagine that there will be members of my own confessional community and those from the wider Protestant tradition as well who will, perhaps, say something of a similar kind regarding my position taken in this essay and the argument made. But I believe that the sacrament of Holy Communion has, throughout much of Protestantism, been diminished to little more than a Zwingli-like memorial meal with little or no impact whatsoever on the lives of those who come together at the Lord's Table.

The sacrament once thought to be the heart and soul of all Christian worship[24] has been replaced by mere human machinations of a dumbed-down liturgical style, looking more like a segment from *That's Entertainment* than the reverential worship of a holy God, or celebrated with so little solemnity and in such a casual manner that it has taken on characteristics to be associated more with "magic" than with "mystery." Let the controversy come, if it will at the same time awaken the church to the very heart and soul of that which is most beautiful and promises to be most fruitful in her liturgical life![25]

For numerous reasons these are extremely difficult days for the Christian church in North America as she faces innumerable challenges on several fronts, including the marginalization of the Church in society; the pressing question of her relevancy in a culture where all forms of science and technology are considered to be definitive; the advent of generations

24. Even though expressed in other words, the following exhortation is representative of a traditional affirmation of the centrality of the Eucharist to Christian worship: "The celebration of the Lord's Supper has ever been regarded by the Church as the innermost sanctuary of the whole Christian worship. We enter here into communion with our Lord and Saviour, Jesus Christ, and do show forth our fellowship with one another as members of his Church." "An Alternate Order of Holy Communion," in Evangelical and Reformed Church, *Hymnal*, 32.

25. While he speaks of the Roman Catholic confession, I find the following observation by James O'Connor applicable to my argument: "It is surely true that the Mystery of the Eucharist can be propounded in such a way that all of the 'shock value' contained in the words of Jesus is removed by anticipation. Such a form of pedagogy or catechesis, however, departs from the approach taken by the Lord himself. It can happen that, by removing the shock, one will remove as well an accurate appreciation of the Eucharist, thereby obviating the response in faith that is necessary to accept Christ's words. . . . Through the centuries the Church has consistently refused to mitigate the shock contained in the words of the Lord. . . . Many have not been able to accept the Mystery as the Church meditated upon it and expounded it more adequately, but their unwillingness or inability has been the occasion used by the Spirit to deepen the Church's appreciation for what Jesus meant." O'Connor, *Hidden Manna*, 96–97.

whose connection to the local church is nowhere near that of their parents or grandparents (even though one could argue the connection of their parents and grandparents was merely conformation to the social norm of the time) and for whom this relationship has been optional as one priority among several others; and the emergence of lifestyles that all but prohibit regular and responsible participation in both the worship and mission of the Church. As stated before, this same environment has been detrimental to the formation and maintenance of Christian identity in any meaningful (and biblical!) sense of the word!

Like any time of "crisis" this one also holds great potential for the Church catholic in general and the local church in particular, which is why this could be a fertile opportunity for the Church to expend energy in the reclamation of what has always made her great, rather than on the pursuit of fashionable and popularly acceptable worship practices as enticements for those who remain "outside" her life; the eucharistic-evangel as union of *Word* and *Sacrament* could be a vital component of that reclamation.[26]

26. "It belongs to the essential life of the Church that it holds to the unity of the Spirit and through Word and Sacrament grows up into the fullness of Christ, that is, built up into complete unity in Him, and extended to the ends of the earth and the ends of the age as the Body of Christ, the fullness of Him that filleth all in all." Torrance, *Conflict and Agreement in the Church*, 1:273.

ONE

The Emmaus Narrative
as Paradigm, Part 1

Beloved in Christ,
the Gospel tells us that on the first day of the week
Jesus Christ was raised from death,
appeared to Mary Magdalene,
on that same day sat at table with two disciples,
and was made known to them in the breaking of the bread.[1]

W E OPEN THIS CHAPTER with an exposition of a biblical pericope from
the Gospel according to St. Luke, chapter 24, verse 13 to the end of
the chapter. Although this particular text is familiar to most Christians,
my interpretation is essentially related to the concern of this essay; to that
extent I deem this pericope to be illustrative or paradigmatic. The rationale
underlying such exposition of this text is (1) my judgment that one of the
fundamental characteristics of this passage is the provocative description,
in narrative style, of the essential liturgical unity of *Word* and *Sacrament* in
Christian worship;[2] and (2) the narrative in its present form portrays initial

1. United Church of Christ, *Book of Worship*, 44.

2. ". . . before this tradition reached Luke, it had been modified by the Eucharistic
liturgy; it follows the sequence of the latter: a reading and explanation of Scripture [vv.
25–27] and the breaking of bread [v. 30]." Stuhlmueller, "The Gospel according to Luke,"
2:162. In an observation that is immediately relevant and profoundly insightful for ecumenical purposes, George Hunsinger writes: "If the Word (Scripture and preaching) is
associated primarily with bearing witness, and the Sacrament (baptism and the Lord's

dismay and confusion concerning the correct identity of Jesus as Christ and the impact of *Word* and *Sacrament* upon correct identification and the consequent transformation and maintenance of a distinctive Christian identity made evident, initially, in the change of disposition in the two disciples from one of despondency to one of delight, followed by renewed energy to share with others (in particular the other followers) the reality of the crucified and risen Christ whose true identity was disclosed in his exposition "of the Scriptures" (Luke 24:32b) and his being "made known to them in the breaking of the bread" (Luke 24:35b). One can comprehend this portrayal through an exploration of the various levels of personal interaction and intricate literary texture located in this pericope. Acknowledgement of the validity of the two observations listed above leads to the conviction that this narrative is illustrative of both the form and content which Christian worship should assume as indicative of its own distinctive liturgical style and reverential character.

The exposition will be guided by the following outline; even though I will not be making specific reference to these headings, they remain the directing principles throughout the process of interpretation of the passage:

1. The unknown presence (Luke 24:16)

2. Expectations in conflict (Luke 24:21a, 27b)

3. The presence and identity disclosed; greater expectations (Luke 24:29–31)

4. Recognition, acknowledgment, and confession (Luke 24:31–33a)

Supper) primarily with mediation, and both with anticipation, then it might be said the Word mediates what it attests, while the Sacrament attests what it mediates, while both anticipate the promised future. The differences would be merely relative. The Sacrament would be visible Word, and the Word audible Sacrament. Moreover, suppose that witness gives us the identity of Jesus Christ, while mediation gives us his presence, and both impart the promised future. If so, then Word and Sacrament would attest Christ's identity, mediate his presence, and anticipate his future, though each in its own way. The difference might be captured, to some extent, as that between hearing and seeing. The Word would have the particular advantage of allowing us to hear that which cannot be seen." Hunsinger, *Eucharist and Ecumenism*, 26.

In a more ecumenical setting, one could reference the work of the Groupe des Dombes in which this ecumenical body affirms the following: "The link between the Word of God as it is heard and the Word of God as it is seen must never be broken in the life of the church, for sacrament is implicit in Word, and Word in sacrament. This is why, 'from the table of both Word of God and the body of Christ, the church unceasingly receives and offers to the faithful the bread of life, especially in the sacred liturgy.'" Clifford, *For the Communion of the Churches*, 84.

5. The transformation of identity, personal and communal (Luke 24:38–53)

Clearly, my intent is not to argue for the historicity of the "Emmaus road" experience; rather, my interest is with the *Sitz im Leben* of Luke and the community to which his gospel is primarily addressed, and in particular the *liturgical Sitz im Leben*!

The narrative opens by telling of two disciples who "that same day" (that is, "the first day of the week") were traveling from Jerusalem to a village named Emmaus. As they traveled together, they were apparently discussing the events of the past several days, including the arrest, condemnation, and death of their master, Jesus of Nazareth. We can surmise from verse 17b ("they stopped walking and looked discouraged") that this conversation was fraught with despair and disappointed expectations. The two disciples traveled away from the gates of the holy city of Jerusalem, where death and despair now prevailed among the followers of Jesus who "were hoping that He was the One who was about to redeem Israel" (v. 21a). From the outset, the narrative creates an atmosphere of disillusionment and a deepening sense of discontent among the followers of Jesus. The words "were hoping" suggest both expectation and disappointment! We should not overestimate, but just as importantly, not *underestimate* the investiture of expectations in Jesus as the promised Messiah—as these early followers understood the identity of the Messiah of God—and the way in which their expectations would impact their own sense of identity as individual disciples and as a community of believers in transition.

The redemption of Israel had been forth-told by prophets and apocalyptic sources of inspiration. The recorded expectations were as multifaceted as were the sources; yet one of the prevailing images throughout such material was that of the messianic expectation. Though even here one must be cautious so as not to give the impression that these messianic expectations were somehow monolithic:

> It has been rightly pointed out that the OT exhibits no clear developments of the messianic expectation . . . the expectation of a Davidic messiah represented only one type of messianism in the period between the exile and A.D. 135. Altogether it took a variety of forms. It was influenced not only by Moses (cf. Deut. 18:15f.) and Elijah (Sir. 48:10) but also in apocalyptic texts and traditions (Eth. Enoch, 2 Esd.) by the idea of a son of man (cf. Dan. 7:13ff.) as a bringer of salvation who was also thought of as preexistent. Even the expectation of a messianic high priest is not lacking . . . no

doubt . . . the messianic hope with which Jesus and the primitive church were faced was anything but unified and unambiguous.[3]

Cognizant of such diversity in messianic expectation, it can still be maintained that the dominant perception of the promised Messiah appears to have been that of one who would arrive on the historical scene with power, might, and wisdom, bringing about the restoration of the glory Israel once had known.[4] Although the developing streams of messianic expectation also appear to have included both the spiritual *and* political dimensions of Israel. As Oscar Cullman concludes: "In the New Testament period the prevailing Messiah type was of course more and more that which we roughly designate the 'political Messiah,' or simply the 'Jewish Messiah' . . . but we must not forget that the expression 'Messiah' was not a *terminus technicus* for this one conception, but was only in the process of becoming that."[5]

The line between the spiritual and political dimensions of messianic expectation was fluid, allowing for some overlap.[6] Nevertheless, the observation I wish to make is (1) the development of messianic expectation (including the themes of redemption and restoration) suggested that with the advent of the Messiah both political and spiritual dimensions of Israel's existence would undergo a *transformation*; and (2) the political dimension of messianic expectation played a *central* role in the thought of the disciples regarding the identity of Jesus:

> Jesus knew very well that all his disciples had the secret hope that he would assume the political Messiah's glorious kingly role. . . . The argument of the sons of Zebedee concerning their rank in the future kingdom is enough to show what thoughts were in the heads of the disciples. Their desertion of their master when he was arrested and their flight was not only the result of understandable human cowardice, but also the result of the disappointment that Jesus did not resemble in the slightest the expected Messiah-king.[7]

It has been contended that, in the context of Luke's narrative, the two disciples "represent all followers of Jesus."[8] Therefore Luke addresses similar

3. Rengstorf, "Jesus Christ," 2:337.

4. Ibid., 334–36.

5. Cullmann, *Christology of the New Testament*, 112.

6. Ibid., 114–16.

7. Ibid., 123–24.

8. Stuhlmueller, "Gospel according to Luke," 2:162.

messianic expectations in the community of faith through these representative voices of the two disciples when he has them say, "But we were hoping that He was the One who was about to redeem Israel" (24:21). "In the
mouth of the disciples on the Emmaus road it is just as much the writer's
attempt to understand Jesus as are the other attempts in the tradition (cf.
Mark 6:14ff.; par. Matt 14:1f.; Luke 9:7f.)."[9] I would simply make the observation that the "writer's attempt to understand Jesus" is also and at the
same time his attempt to address a similar conundrum in the life of the
community of faith to which his gospel is written.

This Jesus of Nazareth, in whom these two disciples (and as representative of similar expectations in the wider community of faith) had
placed such great store as the promised Messiah, had by all *outward* appearances failed to fulfill the content of a particular strain of messianic
expectation.[10] The description of Jesus as "a Prophet powerful in action and
speech" (24:19) would imply that, at best, the impression Jesus had made
on these two disciples was merely that of the expected "prophet."[11] Even
so, one must take into consideration how such a description follows on the
heels of the graphic suffering and horrible death of Jesus; it would seem that
such suffering and shameful death were not considered viable components
of their messianic expectation. The messianic expectation held by the two
(representative) disciples had not been realized in and through the life of
Jesus of Nazareth. Instead, his mission and ministry evidently came into
conflict with such an expectation, because Jesus had been "handed over to
be sentenced to death, and crucified" (24:20). Apparently, with the arrest
and crucifixion of Jesus, the expectation held by his followers had been
dismantled, if not smashed; that is to say, their hopes that this particular
person was the long-awaited Messiah.

While traveling toward Emmaus the two disciples "were discussing
everything that had taken place" (24:14). "And while they were discussing
and arguing, Jesus Himself came near and began to walk along with them.
But they were prevented [literally, "their eyes were prevented"] from recognizing Him" (24:15–17). The reference to the lack of recognition should
not be attributed to some malady of vision; it is better understood as interpreted by the biblical scholar Leon-Dufour when he writes: "the eye is

9. Rengstorf, "Jesus Christ," 2:342.

10. Stuhlmueller, "Gospel according to Luke," 2:162.

11. Cullmann, *Christology of the New Testament*, 13ff. (esp. 22). See also Schnelle,
Theology of the New Testament, 146–48.

identified with the heart in order to point to the spirit which lays hold of something."[12]

The observation made by Leon-Dufour implies that in "heart" and "spirit" the two disciples were unable to lay hold of the identity of their traveling companion; even though familiarity should have brought immediate recognition, Luke's narrative dramatizes the fact that to the disciples Jesus was a stranger.[13] It raises the question, why might that be the case? I would contend that it is a stylistic way of demonstrating just how deeply the "heart" and "spirit" of the two disciples have been informed and shaped by a particular messianic expectation, that is, that of the Messiah-king; more than any other, their expectation of *Jesus* as the promised Messiah had been conditioned by this particular messianic conceptualization. That would of necessity imply that following his suffering, crucifixion and burial they would not have expected to see Jesus again, at least not until the general resurrection of the dead as prelude to the advent of God's coming kingdom of consummation. While the substance of some forms of messianic expectation may have included anticipation of a general resurrection of the dead, there would have been no expectation of an isolated and individual case—even that of the Messiah himself.

The conversational exchange which follows closely on the heels of this encounter with Jesus is possibly the most intriguing aspect of the entire narrative. Having been questioned by Jesus regarding the "things" that had taken place in Jerusalem over the course of the last several days, the disciples begin to tell the "story" of the identity of Jesus (24:19b–24!). Both the form and substance of this portion of the pericope is so captivating because it resembles a covert proclamation of the gospel of the crucified and risen Messiah, which becomes the standard confessional form in the nascent Christian community.[14] The "story" told by these two is in fact the very same narrative which affirms both the true identity of the Messiah

12. Leon-Dufour, *Dictionary of the New Testament*, 186.

13. As Luke Timothy Johnson has observed: Luke ". . . provides a subtly shaded interpretation of the *mode* of Jesus' presence to humans after his resurrection; he can really appear in the guise of a stranger on the road in the midst of human dialogue; he can be recognized in the ritual gestures of the community fellowship meal." Johnson, *Gospel of Luke*, 398.

14. "In a remarkably down-to-earth fashion, Luke shows us narratively the process by which the first believers actually did learn to understand the significance of the events they had witnessed, and to resolve the cognitive dissonance between their experience and their convictions. The resurrection shed new light on Jesus' death, on his words, and on the Scriptures." Ibid., 399.

and that which they apparently have difficulty believing! Interestingly they share this "story" with their travel companion with a sense of obvious disappointment and disillusionment, telling the account as if it were "nothing more than a story" that now had little or no immediate influence on their lives.

The "report" of the women (24:22) "astounded" them, which would imply that they were surprised and confounded by such a report—and not simply because it was women who bore the testimony; rather, it was a questionable ending to a "story" that had already "ended" on Calvary!

And so it would seem that they tell the "story" to the one whose life was the embodiment of the same; apparently without knowing it at the time, they rehearse the true identity of the Messiah with the true Messiah!

This aspect of the passage functions to dramatize both the intensity of disappointed expectation and the consequent inability to properly identify Jesus of Nazareth as Israel's promised Messiah. The response of Jesus lends credibility to this postulate: "He said to them, 'How unwise and slow you are to believe in your hearts all that the prophets have spoken! Didn't the Messiah have to suffer these things and enter into His glory?' Then beginning with Moses and all the Prophets, He interpreted for them the things concerning Himself in all the Scriptures" (24:25–27). The phrase translated above as "unwise" literally means lacking sense, which also has the connotation of being "unintelligent."[15] Not to be read pejoratively, the implication is more that the disciples lack understanding, as a full and comprehensive perspective on the teachings of Scripture concerning the Messiah. Their "eyes" remain unilluminated because their "hearts" have not yet been enlightened by "all that the prophets have spoken" (note the implicit reference to the illuminating characteristic of Scripture as *Word*!). Therefore, they fail to "see" (as in recognize) Jesus Messiah in their presence!

The phrase "(how) slow you are to believe in your hearts" is intended to reinforce the first claim (i.e., "unwise"). Once again the insight of Leon-Dufour is most helpful: "In the N.T., the word ('heart') sometimes indicates . . . the source of one's inmost intellectual intentions (very close to 'spirit': Gk. *Nous*), of faith . . . (and) understanding . . . the center of decisive choices."[16]

The second phrase serves to interpret and further illuminate the intent of the first claim! The two disciples lack "understanding" and a "heart"

15. Leon-Dufour, *Dictionary of the New Testament*, 199.
16. Ibid., 222.

which can lay hold of the full identity of Jesus as Messiah because their "hearts" have been shaped and informed by messianic expectations too severely restricted by images which portend power, might, and glory in the narrowest sense of the terms (i.e., images associated with the Messiah-king).

It would seem that the correction of this misperception, or better, misunderstanding of identity is initiated with the phrase, "Then beginning with Moses and all the Prophets, He interpreted for them the things concerning Himself in all the Scriptures" (24:27). The phrasing of the comment discloses the *exact* nature of the dilemma for the two disciples (and of course, through them, as representative of the entire community, for all believers addressed by Luke's gospel account) who have adhered to a particular and limited messianic expectation. That is to say, even their reading of Moses, all the Prophets, and the whole of the Scriptures has been guided by a restrictive hermeneutic; the first order of business, therefore, is to provide them with a much broader perspective and more holistic hermeneutic in order to enlarge their panoramic view of the promised Messiah. Rather than focus on any one section of the Scriptures, in offering the most reliable and richest validation of his identity as Messiah, Jesus employs a hermeneutic which is inclusive of the "whole counsel of God" as found in the Hebrew Scriptures. The identity of the Messiah is of such importance and of such magnitude for both the individual believer and the entire community that one must not rely upon a kind of "proof-text" methodology in the scriptural search for the Messiah as the One *God* had promised and defined!

I would also draw the reader's attention to that wonderful turn of a phrase (i.e., "the things concerning Himself") which picks up a similar phrase found earlier in this periscope; Cleopas says to Jesus, "Are You the only visitor to Jerusalem who doesn't know *the things* that happened there in these days?" To which Jesus replies, "What *things*?" And they say, "*The things* concerning Jesus the Nazarene . . ." (24:18–19; emphasis mine). This literary devise unites the two forms of messianic expectation: the one offered by the two disciples (24:19–24) and that which is now offered by Jesus himself as he "interpreted" the whole of the Scriptures (24:25–27). In this manner the "things concerning Jesus the Nazarene" are brought into greater harmony with the fuller interpretation of the Scriptures provided by Jesus (24:27!); the narrative rendition of the identity of "Jesus the Nazarene" (24:19–27) is now given a holistic biblical warrant as the fulfillment of the identity "Jesus the Nazarene" as the promised Messiah; this is a stunning reinterpretation of messianic expectation which highlights the whole of his life *and* death ("Didn't the Messiah have to suffer these *things* . . . [24:26]; notice the use of "things" once again!).

The entire life of Jesus becomes the hermeneutical key that unlocks the deepest dimensions of the mystery as located in the whole of the Scriptures of "the things concerning Himself." This narrative reinterpretation of messianic expectation can be seen as the desire to bring such a holistic perspective to bear upon the present experience and expectation of the two disciples, and the consequence of such is a transformation of their expectation and lives ("Weren't our hearts ablaze within us while He was talking with us on the road and explaining the Scriptures to us?" [24:32]). Now their expectation falls in line with the Messiah *God* had promised to send, and even his ignominious death took on a whole new meaning in light of the interpretation/explanation Jesus offered them: "The . . . positive significance of Jesus dying becomes evident. . . . It consisted of the fact that his dying belonged to God's plan of salvation. It was said to the disciples along the road to Emmaus who thought in their resignation, 'But we had hoped that he was the one to redeem Israel' (Luke 24:21), 'Was it not necessary that the Christ should suffer these things and enter into his glory' (Luke 24:26)."[17]

However, it is not until later in the narrative structure that we are given any indication of the transformative effects which this reinterpretation and expansion of messianic expectation had upon the personal identities and lives of the two disciples. It was the death of Jesus which posed the most extreme obstacle for these two disciples,[18] and now, rather than an obstacle, this same death becomes of central importance to the identity of the Christ; this once significant hindrance to the disciples' identification of Jesus as Messiah, is given "positive significance" through the interpretive technique of Jesus himself (i.e., the Word's self-disclosure!). The death of Jesus is now perceived to be of fundamental importance to his identity as that which "belongs to God's plan of salvation." I read this as indicative of the way in which Jesus, as *the* Word of God, is always, and under the power of the Holy Spirit, offering himself—that is to say, his true identity

17. Goppelt, *Theology of the New Testament*, 2:283.

18. "In antiquity, crucifixion was seen as the most horrible and most shameful way to die. It certainly was believed that such a death showed a person so put to death had sinned gravely and had been abandoned by God. Indeed, even some of Jesus' disciples came to this very conclusion [see Luke 24:20–21!]. Death by crucifixion was a scandal for anyone, any family, any group of followers of a great figure." Witherington, *Indelible Image*, 1:612.

(read: "real presence")—to the members of his body, the Church. All other expectations of who Jesus was, is, or will be for us pale by comparison to the identity we are given in and through the living Word of God, and the witness to the Word of God (i.e., Scripture, *primarily*, and Proclamation, *secondarily*).

"So they said to each other, 'Weren't our hearts ablaze within us while He was talking with us on the road and explaining the Scriptures to us?'" (24:32) This affirmation and acknowledgment of both insight gained, and the beginnings of some form of spiritual stirring, follows the account of the breaking of bread and consequent recognition of the risen Christ Jesus. The voices of the disciples, as a literary technique employed by Luke, allude to the beginning of what I have called a transformative process. Jesus has first interpreted the Scriptures in such a manner that the "hearts" (recall the relationship drawn between "hearts" and "understanding") of the two are "ablaze" with a deeper and more penetrating comprehension of the identity of Jesus as the fulfillment of a holistic messianic expectation. The comprehensive interpretation of the Scriptures generates an opening of the "heart" to the multifaceted levels of messianic expectation embodied in the fullness of the Hebrew Scriptures. This account is paradigmatic of the initial stage in recognition and transformation, that is, the combination of interpretation and proclamation of the Scriptures within the context of an encounter with the risen Christ where, while "at table with them . . . He took the bread, blessed and broke it, and gave it to them" (24:30) becomes the catalyst for "their eyes [to be] opened" (24:21).

This interpretation of the Scriptures, as a comprehensive approach to identification of the Messiah in fulfillment of a holistic messianic expectation, initiates the process of recognition. The opening of the "eyes" and initial awakening of the "heart" through such interpretation, in union with the act of Christ taking, blessing, breaking, and giving the bread to the two, eventuates in the acknowledgment of the crucified Jesus as risen and living, leading to the fuller confession of the true identity of Jesus as the promised Messiah (24:34–35!). Therefore, the priority of the transformative process is given to the comprehensive interpretation of the scriptural messianic expectation in the proper identification of Jesus of Nazareth—the crucified one—as, in fact, the fulfillment of God's promise and the Messiah. This particular transformation of the "heart" and "eyes" (as the ability to lay hold of the true identity of Jesus of Nazareth as Messiah), including a fuller understanding and inclusion of suffering and death as essential to that same identity, anticipates the transformation of the identity of the disciple who will one day confess, in the words of the Apostle Paul, "I no longer live, but Christ lives in me" (Gal 2:20a).

Furthermore, this hermeneutical event makes possible a greater degree of receptivity to the encounter about to transpire, an encounter that will dramatically crystallize the truth of the interpretation Jesus has given of "the things concerning Himself" (24:27). The interpretation of the Scriptures sets in motion the proper identification of Jesus Messiah; the "eyes" of the two disciples—and through the reading of this same narrative, the "eyes" of the community of faith gathered about the altar table—are prepared, if you will, for the revelation about to be given at table. This stage in the process of recognition will enable the two disciples (and the gathered community) to lay hold of the true identity of the crucified and risen One now made present as the promised Messiah, and to do so with their "hearts" (recalling as we should that the "heart" is often, though not in every case, symbolic of intellect, will, volition, and personality).

This section of the narrative—which opens with an atmosphere of disappointment and discouragement, with the disciples' apparent confusion concerning the identity of Jesus of Nazareth, including the interpretation of the Scriptures by Jesus himself—is analogous to the reading and interpretation of the *Word* in the ongoing liturgical life of the Christian community (e.g., Acts 2:42; 13:15–41; 20:7, 11; 28:30). Stated even more boldly, the interpretation which Jesus brings to bear on the messianic expectation of the two disciples, and through the narration of this account within the context of the Church's liturgy, is brought to bear on similar expectations held by members of the faith community and is therefore analogous to the event of proclamation which transpires in the worshipping community itself. In this fashion the narrative *Sitz im Leben* of the two disciples in the gospel illuminates the liturgical *Sitz im Leben* of other disciples in the wider community of faith. This gospel narrative is far more than an account of the confused messianic expectations of two disciples en route to Emmaus; it is also and at the same time a dramatic disclosure of the transformative power of the *Word* and paradigmatic of all followers who struggle with the identification of this Jesus of Nazareth, who was crucified, as the promised Messiah of Israel.

The Scriptures, when interpreted holistically (as in the "whole counsel of God"), impacting as they do both the expectations held by believers and the identities shaped by such expectations, become the *Word* proclaimed ("real presence"), which illuminates the "hearts" and "eyes" of the members of the faith community at worship; together with the "breaking of bread," this liturgical event becomes the most fertile soil for the revelation of the true identity of Jesus Christ and the receptivity of his "real presence" as Host, as Prophet and Priest, as Offering and the One to Offer the Sacrifice of Satisfaction/Expiation/Propitiation, as Lord and King of this proleptic feast awaiting future fulfillment.[19]

In the following chapter we will continue to pursue this same theme and pericope, but the focus will be more intentionally on the "sacramental" aspect of the liturgy and transformative process, that is, the Eucharist.

19. ". . . while it may be the eucharist that fulfills the church, it is Holy Scripture that establishes it. The church lives by the freedom of grace, through the proclamation of the Word of God, or it does not live at all. The Reformed will stand for the centrality of Christ, as attested by Holy Scripture, and for the wind of the Spirit to blow where it will. A preaching office without its Eucharistic compliment in the weekly liturgy, however, would be like a head without a torso, while a sacramental priestly office without a robust liturgy of the Word would be much the reverse." Hunsinger, *Eucharist and Ecumenism*, 325.

TWO

The Emmaus Narrative as Paradigm, Part 2

According to Luke,
when our risen Lord was at table with his disciples,
he took the bread, blessed and broke it,
and gave it to them.
Then their eyes were opened
and they recognized him.[1]

A S WAS STATED IN the last chapter, the breaking of bread in the Lucan account (chapter 24) serves to crystallize the truth of the interpretation of the Scriptures which Jesus had expounded "concerning Himself." The interpretation of the Scriptures (as the *Word* of God proclaimed, that is, the "real presence") is fundamental to the process of recognition, acknowledgment, and ultimate confession of the identity of Jesus Messiah, just as the taking, blessing, breaking, and offering of the bread (as "visible" *Word* in its sacramental form) discloses the true identity and therefore the *real presence* of the crucified and risen Jesus of Nazareth as the Christ of God. This event in turn is crucial to the transformation of the identity of the disciples;[2] transformation of both individual and communal identity is based on a proper comprehension and identification of Jesus of Nazareth

1. Presbyterian Church USA, *Book of Common Worship*, 68.
2. "He transforms into himself those whom he nourishes with his substance." De Lubac, *Corpus Mysticum*, 178.

31

as the Christ: "To recognize Jesus as the Christ is not a matter of objective ascertaining. This recognition calls for a fundamental *metanoia* in which the whole of the person who recognizes Jesus as the Christ is transformed. In other words, to recognize Jesus as the Christ is at the same time a new self-understanding in and through a renewal of life."[3] The death of Jesus is integrated into the overall program of messianic expectation—first, through the interpretation of the Scriptures (i.e., as the spoken *Word*), and secondly through the breaking of bread (i.e., as the visible *Word*).[4] The messianic expectation that shaped the identification of Jesus of Nazareth and that of the disciple(s) is itself thereby transformed: "The disciple of a powerful Messiah-king is quite different from the disciple of one condemned to death!"[5]

One of the more telling passages of this Lucan narrative reads: "It was as He reclined at table with them that He took the bread, blessed and broke it, and gave it to them. Then their eyes were opened, and they recognized Him, but He disappeared from their sight" (Luke 24:30–31).

One cannot help noticing the similarity between this particular language and that found in the narrative account of the Passover meal that Jesus shared with his disciples (see Luke 22:14–20).[6] In advance of his actual

3. Schillebeeckx, *Interim Report on the Books Jesus & Christ*, 23.

4. "The indissoluble link between Word and sacrament is based on the mystery of the Word made flesh, for Christ is himself both Word and sacrament. The specific character of each stems from the complementarity of speaking and acting in human living. They correspond concretely to the two different states of the church's constitution and mission. In the New Testament the ministry of Jesus Christ and the apostles attests that the proclaimed Word is the source of the calling and gathering of the people of God . . . [the] sacrament accompanies and fulfills the Word by carrying out in action the gift of God proclaimed by the Word." Clifford, *For the Communion of the Churches*, 84.

5. Cullmann, *The Christology of the New Testament*, 23.

6. "During the course of the [Passover] meal at which He instituted the Eucharist, Christ uttered the traditional words of the liturgy: 'Blessed art Thou, O Lord, Our God, King of the earth, who hast given to Thy people Israel this season of festivity for joy and for a memorial' (*le-zikkaron*). Each item of food had its own significance. As they ate them the Jews could re-live mystically, *sacramentally*, the events of the deliverance and Exodus from Egypt. They became contemporaries of their forefathers and were saved with them. There was in the mystery of the paschal meal a kind of telescoping of two periods of history, the present and the Exodus. The past event became present or rather each person became a contemporary of the past event. The unity of the redemptive act of the Lord was affirmed by this celebration. It is this mystery of redemptive act accomplished once for all and yet ever renewed, present and applied, the church came to designate by the word *musterion* or *sacramentum*. The sacramental mystery belongs both to the Judaic and the Christian tradition and expresses the biblical meaning of the

death, this meal, including the "breaking of bread" and the "sharing of the cup," prefigures the full and proper identification of Jesus as the promised Messiah:

> Jesus' life is oriented to that hour in which he will no longer have disposition over himself (in the passion); but (in the Eucharist) he can have control in advance precisely over this being a passive object of another's disposition (i.e. in the sense of the divinely willed pouring forth of himself). Toward this, his whole anxious (Luke 12:50) longing is directed (Luke 22:15). Even the simple formula of the words of institution shows the coincidence of disposing and being disposed: "This is my body which is given for you" (Luke 22:19), "this is my blood . . . which is poured out for you" (Luke 14:24). The "being given" points, as the "being poured out" shows even more clearly, to the passion and crucifixion. If the primitive church and Paul with it will conclude from the fact of the resurrection of Jesus to the universal salvific significance of the cross (which had to remain unrecognizable in the process itself)—it was because this truth as "sacred-public mystery" was already evident in the gestures with which Jesus at table shared his flesh and blood as given and poured. The gesture of self-giving lies temporally ahead of the violent events of the passion and thereby shows that it is also the ontological reason why the gruesome events following could gain universal salvific significance. . . . The humanity of Jesus—his "flesh and blood" or his "life"—is thus, even from the incarnation, eucharistically determined, inasmuch as it is the bodily gift of God to the world. The realization of this giving in the Last Supper, passion, and resurrection is only the execution of this gift long since intended and really established and begun.[7]

However, within the form and flow of the present narrative structure (i.e., Luke 24:30), this idiom becomes the vehicle for expressing a disclosure of the identity of the crucified and risen Jesus of Nazareth as the promised Messiah; suffering and death are integral to the identity of God's promised Messiah.[8] In its literary context this event unites the meal shared by

---

salvation-history which was accomplished in time *once for all* but which is equally *present* at all times *by Word and Sacrament.*" Thurian, *The Eucharistic Memorial*, 1:19.

7. Balthasar, *The Von Balthasar Reader*, 282–83.

8. "The incarnation is not merely a Christmas event. To be man is a process of becoming man; Jesus' manhood grew throughout his earthly life, finding its completion in the supreme moment of the incarnation, his death, resurrection and exaltation. Only then is the incarnation fulfilled to the very end. And so we must say that the incarnation of the Son itself redeems us. This mystery of Christ or of redemption we can call,

Jesus with his twelve disciples "on the night when He was betrayed" (1 Cor 11:23b) with the present experience of the two disciples "as He reclined at table with them" (Luke 24:30a). The similarity of both meals as disclosure events of Jesus' true identity as the Christ of God is enhanced by Luke's use of the formula, "[Jesus] took the bread, blessed and broke it, and gave it to them" (Luke 24:30b)—a formula resonating with that of the Passover meal Jesus shared with the twelve: "And [Jesus] took bread, gave thanks, broke it, gave it to them . . ." (Luke 22:19a). Both the breaking (i.e., the "fraction")[9] and the giving are symbolic of the suffering and death of Jesus as fundamental characteristics of *his* messianic identity.

The two disciples suddenly "recognize" Jesus because (1) this event at table in Emmaus reflects the event of the Passover meal held prior to the arrest, trial, crucifixion, and resurrection of Jesus; and (2) the similarity between the two related experiences crystallizes the interpretation of the Scriptures given earlier (Luke 4:26) in the narrative. Furthermore, the "breaking of the bread" symbolizes the wounds inflicted in the flagellation and crucifixion of Jesus, and such wounds are now employed by Jesus in his self-identification as the crucified and risen Messiah. Later in this same narrative, when Jesus appears to his gathered disciples (as representative of the gathered community), he identifies himself by reference to his wounds (Luke 24:39)![10] In each case, Jesus takes the initiative in the revelatory

---

in its totality, a mystery of saving worship; a mystery of praise (the upward movement) and of salvation (the downward movement)." Schillebeeckx, *Christ, the Sacrament of the Encounter with God*, 19.

9. "In the Eucharist, in all our eucharistic liturgies, there is one moment called the fraction or breaking of the bread when the bread is divided for the communion of all." Thurian, *Visible Unity and Tradition*, 136. Max Thurian is to be applauded for drawing attention to the symbolic meaning of this liturgical moment (beyond the profound symbolism of the body of Christ broken and given for our salvation) in the current situation of divided churches as both "a particular pang of sorrow for our division" but also and at the same time "a sign of our hope." Ibid. This is a particularly important and salient insight if we acknowledge that whenever and wherever the Eucharist is celebrated in the Church, it is both a visible sign of the brokenness we mourn at present and a sign of the promise of ever greater visible unity wherever Christians are willing to be "broken" for the sake of ecumenical growth in grace.

10. "It is fully consistent, therefore, that in Jesus' statements about his suffering, the announcement of his death is always accompanied by that of his resurrection. This is not so much intended to discredit the opponents who refused to believe him and delivered him up to death on the cross (cf. Luke 24:26 with 24:19ff.). One should not, therefore, underestimate the fact that the resurrection event, however it may be interpreted historically, has its proper place in Jesus' messiahship." Rengstorf, "Jesus Christ," 2:240.

event, just as he had taken the initiative with the two disciples on the road to Emmaus in opening the Scriptures. It is, therefore, the initiative of God in Christ and under the illuminating power of the Holy Spirit which makes both the interpretation of Scripture (i.e., the spoken *Word*) and the sacramental meal (i.e., the visible *Word*) a fundamental revelatory encounter with the true Jesus Messiah. This is why I stress the necessity for the unity of *Word* and *Sacrament* in the *Eucharistic-Evangel*, as both form the matrix essential to the full, true identity (i.e., "real presence") of Christ.[11]

The depth of receptivity on the part of the disciples (both "eyes" and "hearts" open to this encounter) is determinative for the process of transformation itself. However, the inverse of this statement is of equal, if not surpassing, importance: the revelatory event itself creates the faith through which receptivity becomes possible, that is, the faith itself as the capacity to receive the disclosure is a gift of God's grace and not a work of human intuition or imagination. Both aspects of the encounter are crucial to the transformation, which lends clarity to the Apostle Paul's exhortation to the Corinthians: "For anyone who eats and drinks without discerning the body eats and drinks judgment upon himself" (1 Cor 11:29). Once the "eyes" of the disciples were opened and they recognized Jesus, then the interpretation of the Scriptures offered by Christ (as a fuller and more comprehensive interpretation of messianic expectation) are seen to have had a deeper and far more profound significance for the identity of the disciples in relation to Jesus of Nazareth. The combined experience of scriptural interpretation (the spoken *Word*) and sacramental action (the visible *Word*), as integral to the identity of Jesus Messiah, serve to strengthen and intensify the transformation of the disciples' self-understanding and identity.[12]

11. Making reference to the experience of the two disciples on the road to Emmaus as paradigmatic, Max Thurian writes: "Having disclosed to them the mystery of the Scriptures as a sensible token of His presence, He recalled to them by the breaking of bread the Eucharist that He instituted as the sacrament of His body and blood. The eucharistic body of Christ was to be another form of His presence to console them and strengthen them in faith. Then 'their eyes were opened, and they knew him; and he vanished out of their sight' (24.31). The disciples were astonished at their own unbelief. They should have recognized Him in His Word as they had now recognized Him in the Sacrament. 'Was not our heart burning within us, while he spake to us in the way, while he opened to us the scriptures . . . and they rehearsed the things that had happened in the way, and how he was known of them in the breaking of the bread' (24:32, 35). Scripture and the Eucharist are two different forms of the presence of the Risen Lord to console them and to strengthen them in their faith by the Holy Spirit." Thurian, *The Eucharistic Memorial*, 1:86–87.

12. "At the end of the story, we find the disciples involved in critical self-reflection:

It is essential to a positive theological affirmation to assert once again the initiative of God in the revelatory encounter with the "spoken" and "visible" *Word*; the grace of God *alone* and the power of the Holy Spirit *alone* make possible the opening of the "eyes" and "heart" of the disciples, bringing about recognition, acknowledgment, and confession. In both "spoken" and "visible" *Word* and under the empowerment of the Holy Spirit, the "real presence" of Jesus Messiah is embraced in the threefold movement of recognition, acknowledgment, and confession.[13] But this is not to say that the revelatory encounter is nothing more than an inner, subjective experience; rather, the experience that creates faith (as the opening of the "eyes" and "heart") unites the *objective* ("real presence" of Jesus Messiah) and the *subjective* (the faith and identity of the disciple) dimensions and dynamics of this encounter.[14] I stress both the initiative of God and the receptivity of the disciples to this disclosure event; for the identity of the disciples to be

---

the interpretation of the scriptures had set their hearts on fire; yet the recognition of the wanderer as the resurrected Christ occurred only at the breaking of the bread. Put alternatively, the disciples recognized Jesus at the breaking of bread; yet this recognition would have been impossible apart from the preceding exposition of the scriptures. . . . Informed by the hearing of the scriptures, the breaking of the bread at Emmaus transforms the disciples into people of faith . . . the story also teaches us that although faith is not the presupposition for companionship (with Christ), it is the anticipated result and a fundamental element in the self-understanding of the Christian community as a people of bread." Vondey, *People of Bread*, 170–71.

13. T. F. Torrance writes this: "This stress upon the action of God in the Sacrament is reflected in the actual rite itself when the emphasis is laid upon the verbs 'broken for you,' 'shed for you,' which are figured and attested by the outward action of the minister. What Christ has commanded to be figured and attested in this active way, He undoubtedly performs, giving His Body and shed Blood for our nourishment, and effectively applying His death and resurrection for our salvation. . . . In Christ's direct action His Word and His Act are absolutely identical and coincident, but in the sacramental mode of operation they are held partially apart in order to make room for personal relations in decision and faith and repentance, and so for the growth of personal communion in union and love." Torrance, *Conflict and Agreement in the Church*, 2:145–46.

14. Paul Tillich once wrote: "God in his self-manifestation to man is dependent on the way man receives his manifestation." Tillich, *Systematic Theology*, 1:61. I have come to appreciate the observation of Wolfgang Vondey:

"Discerning the bread means to recognize in the breaking and sharing of the bread the continuing presence of Christ and as a consequence the possibility of and responsibility for creating and sustaining the unity of the Church. It is an exercise that seeks to recognize the presence of Christ in the other and thereby acknowledges the other as a member of the one body. This exercise is a fundamental ecumenical endeavor. It is as much a theological undertaking as it is an emotional, psychological, ethical, and social responsibility." Vondey, *People of the Bread*, 232.

transformed (and conformed!) to that of their Master, such identity must occur under the influence of the Christ's full (i.e., true) identity disclosed as both "spoken" and "visible" *Word*.

The crucial component of receptivity on the part of the disciples is manifested in their plea to Jesus at the moment (in the narrative) he appears to be parting company with them: "Stay with us," they say, "because it's almost evening, and now the day is almost over" (Luke 24:29a). Note the reference to the approaching darkness ("it's almost evening"), which could be Luke's way of contrasting the darkness of the disciples' understanding with the light of Jesus' illuminating interpretation of the Scriptures while they were still in transit. Apparently, these two distraught disciples have a strong desire to hear more from their traveling companion; as literary device, Luke intimates that the disciples desire even further illumination at the end of the day. This plea for Jesus' presence and continuing illumination further discloses a level of receptivity on the part of the disciples, because "Jesus really would have departed . . . (and) . . . without him, darkness would have descended."[15] Had Jesus departed from the disciples at that point, the disclosure of his true identity would have remained partial at best, based on the interpretation of Scripture yet lacking the further enrichment of the eucharistic moment!

The encounter with the true identity ("real presence") of Jesus as the Messiah of God, disclosed as both "spoken" and "visible" *Word*, is evident the following characteristics of the narrative:

(1) Where once the two disciples were in despair and uncertain as to the true identity of Jesus as the promised Messiah of God (Luke 24:21), the one whose suffering and death had brought their own identities (as "followers") into question, following this encounter (through the opening of the Scriptures and the breaking of bread), the same two are portrayed as willing and able to joyfully return to Jerusalem (the place of crucifixion!) with the "Word of Life" (Luke 24:33, 35):

> Anyone who at first took offense at the arrest and death of Jesus and then proclaimed him as the sole and universal bringer of salvation must unmistakably have undergone a change: he has been converted, and this is a historically demonstrable fact. A process of conversion, from disenchantment with Jesus to *metanoia* and recognition that he indeed was and is . . . the redeemer of the world,

---

15. Stuhlmueller, "The Gospel according to Luke," 2:163.

the Christ . . . must thus be accepted historically if this change is to be in some way comprehensible as a historical fact.[16]

The two now recognize that the one who interpreted the Scriptures with such conviction and force—thereby opening their "eyes" and "hearts" to a more holistic pattern of messianic expectation—this one who also and at table took the bread, blessed, broke, and gave it to them as their guest, this is the very same crucified Jesus of Nazareth. It hardly seems beyond the realm of possibility that, as Jesus engaged in this action at table, the gaze of the two would quite naturally have been drawn to his hands and wrists, and it would have been impossible not to notice the prominent presence of nail marks![17] The sorrowful "story" of Jesus with which the two were painfully familiar (Luke 24:19–24!), a story which told of the identity of Jesus and shaped the self-identification of the disciples is—following the encounter with the risen Christ Jesus—perceived as synonymous with the interpretation of the Scriptures he himself had offered on the road. In this way the once sorrowful "story" becomes the "story" of victory over sin and death, one of hope beyond hope. Now it is *this* story that embodies the fulfillment of messianic expectation, and it is *this* crucified and risen Jesus, himself the embodiment of the "story," whose presence instigates the transformation of identity in his disciples.

(2) When the two disciples return to their brethren in Jerusalem, they rehearse the experience of their encounter with the crucified and risen Jesus of Nazareth; the "story" they formally recounted with an attitude of incredulity (see Luke 24:22!) is now told to the gathered community as the "gospel truth"! Moreover, when they are informed (Luke 24:34) that "the Lord has certainly been raised," their response (Luke 24:35) would imply that they had no problem believing this testimony. The two who were once in bondage to disillusionment and despair are now (together with the community of faith) rejoicing; they have been gifted with faith in Jesus of Nazareth as the crucified and risen One who fulfills all messianic expectation. They have been gifted with a new (transformed) identity, an identity which is now defined by the revelation of the true Messiah of God and shaped by

16. Schillebeeckx, *Interim Report on the Books Jesus & Christ*, 76–77.

17. "It is difficult not to be reminded of the presence of Christ, interceding in heaven and present in glory with the signs of His passion on our behalf, signs which are the wounds of the nails in His hands uplifted in intercession. We ourselves are marked with the cross by the sacraments, which are mysteries of death and resurrection with Christ . . . In this reciprocity or exchange we are perfectly united to Him. . . ." Thurian, *The Eucharistic Memorial*, 1:36.

their new comprehension of the way in which messianic expectation has been fulfilled in the life story of Jesus.

What has been said of the two disciples on the road to Emmaus is applicable to the entire community of faith as well; within the structure of Luke's narrative, the two are considered to be representative of all followers of Jesus: "When it represented itself as the community of Jesus, the primitive church intended to represent itself simply as the messianic community. For in its preaching of Jesus as messiah it was at the same time interpreting itself messianically in relation to its life, its historical origins and aims."[18]

In its present form Luke's narrative places the breaking of bread at the center as the climax of the story and revelatory encounter with the crucified and risen Jesus Messiah. In the breaking of bread the true identity of the crucified and risen Jesus of Nazareth, as the promised Messiah whose story embodies the fullness of messianic expectation "in all the Scriptures," is given comprehensive expression. Therefore, in this event, the interpretation of the Scriptures and the breaking of bread, Jesus is "present" in the fullness of his personal identity. With the breaking of bread the interpretation of the Scriptures ("concerning Himself") takes on the deepest and most profound significance for the lives of his followers in the community of faith being formed in his image as Messiah.[19] Together, the interpretation of the Scriptures "concerning Himself" and the "breaking of bread" become the paradigmatic liturgical matrix for the transformation of identity on both personal and corporate levels. It is the encounter with the true identity of Jesus Christ (i.e., the revelation of his "real presence") as the crucified and risen Messiah which makes possible this radical, conversional transformation of the identity of the disciple as well as the community of faith gathered in Christ's name:

> In the course of these worship services, in which bread was broken "with glad and generous hearts" (Acts 2:26), the presence of the risen Christ was experienced ever anew as a reality. The goal of

18. Rengstorf, "Jesus Christ," 2:339.

19. Max Thurian offers this insight: "Thus the Risen Lord appeared unto His own under very different human forms, and they failed to recognize Him except by His word or by an action peculiar to Himself. It was as if Christ wished to accustom His disciples to see Him in their neighbor, in their brothers and in the Church. The Church, which is the society of men attached to the Lord and which reproduces His Word and actions, is truly the body of Christ and the sign of His living presence. These visible signs are diverse in form, and in their efficacy, but they all call attention to the presence of Christ to convey that presence to mankind." Thurian, *The Eucharistic Memorial*, 1:87.

these services was precisely the realization of fellowship with the same risen Christ who had appeared to his assembled disciples at the meal on Easter Sunday. . . . The "appearance meals," if we may call them that, helped the early Church to experience always afresh the presence of the Lord even if not so tangibly as he was experienced during the "forty days" after Easter.[20]

The distinctively liturgical format (i.e., the interpretation of Scriptures and breaking of bread) is, under the power of the Holy Spirit, a disclosure event of the distinctive identity of Jesus Christ (i.e., the "real presence") as the crucified and risen Messiah, which makes possible the transformation and creation of a distinctive Christian identity:

> Thus Christian faith is a remembrance of the life and death of the risen Jesus through acting in accordance with his example—not through imitating what he did, but, like Jesus, through allowing an intense experience of God to have an influence on our own new situation. Christian life can and must be a remembrance of Jesus . . . (and) . . . the story of Jesus . . . experienced as the illuminating and transforming symbol.[21]

A careful exegetical investigation of Luke 24:33–52 discloses a similar pattern where both the "spoken *Word*" and the "visible *Word*" lend clarity to the true identity of the crucified and risen Jesus Messiah. The important distinction to be made between the two narrative sections (i.e., vv. 13–32 and vv. 33–52) is that in the latter section the order of scriptural interpretation and self-disclosure is reversed. In the latter section (Luke 24:33–52), Jesus reveals his wounds first (e.g., v. 39) and only after having eaten speaks of the manner in which he has fulfilled "everything written about Himself in the law of Moses and the prophets and the psalms" (Luke 24:44). Once more Jesus refers to the full body of the Hebrew Scriptures (i.e., the Law, the Prophets, and the Writings; the "whole counsel of God") when speaking of his having fulfilled "everything written about Himself" as the promised Messiah. When the text says of Jesus that he then "opened their minds to understand the Scriptures" (Luke 24:45), this is certainly not intended to suggest that Jesus went book by book, verse by verse, "proof-texting" his claim to having fulfilled messianic expectation! Rather:

---

20. Cullmann, *The Christology of the New Testament*, 208.

21. Schillebeeckx, *Interim Report on the Books Jesus & Christ*, 54, 60.

> The title [Messiah] expresses a continuity between the task [Je-
> sus] had to fulfill and the Old Testament. The Messiah represents
> the fulfillment of the role of mediation which the whole of God's
> chosen people should have realized . . . the Messiah comprehends
> and fulfills the whole history of Israel . . . therefore, the idea of the
> Messiah is important to the extent that it establishes a continuity
> between the work of Jesus and the mission of the chosen people
> of Israel.[22]

In this sense only does Jesus speak of having fulfilled the Scriptures!

The conclusion to this portion of the narrative states that "[the disciples and followers of Jesus] returned to Jerusalem with great joy, and were
continually in the temple blessing God" (Luke 24:52–53). A rather startling
claim, and a clear manifestation of a transformation of their former identities; the experience of transformation parallels that of the two disciples
on the road to Emmaus: "On the basis of their encounters with the risen
Jesus, the disciples finally answered (the question of the Messiah as the
earthly Jesus) by the confession that he was the Messiah and that in him
God has fulfilled his promise to the house of David and Israel of salvation
for the whole of mankind in a manner that is nevertheless only accessible to
faith."[23] This "faith"—which is both a byproduct of the liturgical encounter
with the crucified and risen Jesus of Nazareth as the promised Messiah, and
the element of receptivity to this revelatory event—serves as the foundation
for the transformation of identity: "To call Jesus 'the Christ' . . . implies a
transformed self-understanding as an element of *metanoia* and renewal of
life. Jesus can never be appropriated as the Christ in a purely . . . objectify-
ing manner. Unless Jesus is 'received' by others in faith, he can never be the
Christ for them."[24]

Finally, there is this crucial observation: The revelation of the true
identity of Jesus as Messiah, through the interpretation of Scriptures and
the breaking of bread, effects transformation of identity which in turn eventuates in mission! For the two disciples in the early portion of the narrative,
the mission is evident in their return to the "city of death" (Jerusalem) with
the proclamation of life and joy! For the gathered community of disciples,
the mission is clearly implied in the words of Jesus himself: "You are witnesses of these things"—and therefore, as "witnesses" they are to pursue

22. Cullmann, *The Christology of the New Testament*, 126–27.

23. Rengstorf, "Jesus Christ," 2:342.

24. Schillebeeckx, *Interim Report on the Books Jesus & Christ*, 342.

the following mission—"that repentance and forgiveness of sins [note the parallel to Jesus' own mission!] should be preached in [Jesus' name] to all nations" (Luke 24:47). The revealed identity of the crucified and risen Jesus Messiah inspires the transformation of the disciples' identities, which in turn is shaped by Jesus' mission determining the identification of their own particular mission:

> Since the Church already experienced Christ's coming to his Church we can also better understand how the early Christians could think of him as both Lord of his Church and Lord over the whole world . . . that Christ is at the same time Lord of this little community which represents his body on earth, and from that very centre Sovereign over all the world. We grasp this when we consider that his lordship is already experienced every time the little community celebrates the Lord's Supper.[25]

The particularity of this mission, in symmetry with that of Jesus Messiah, is primarily one of being, as the Apostle Paul would write, "ambassadors for Christ" (2 Cor 5:20); and even more pointedly the mission itself Paul would define in the clearest of terms: ". . . certain that God is appealing through us. We plead on Christ's behalf, 'Be reconciled to God.' He made the One who did not know sin to be sin for us, so that we might become the righteousness of God in Him" (2 Cor 5:20b). The transformative power of the encounter with the "real presence" of Christ shapes and even necessitates a mission that is substantively one of "reconciliation" (defined *theologically* and not politically) of the world beyond the boundaries of the church. And yet the need to reunite the brethren is itself a direct result of the encounter with the true identity of Jesus Messiah. The foundation of both "church" and "mission" is located in the reality of the "real presence" of Jesus Christ, and made possible only under the influence of the Holy Spirit; this is an *ecumenical* mission![26]

25. Cullmann, *The Christology of the New Testament*, 212–13.

26. T. F. Torrance writes: "The whole relation between Christ and His Church, Christ in the Church and the Church in Christ, needs to be understood much more from the perspective of reconciliation, in terms of *Christus pro nobis*. In the words of the Lund Report: 'What concerns Christ concerns His Body also. What has happened to Christ uniquely in His once and for all death and resurrection on our behalf, happens also to the Church in its way as His Body . . . so that the way of Christ is the way of His Body.' . . . . We must think of Christ entering upon His active ministry as true God and true Man in one Person, in a union which penetrated into our sinful humanity and created room for itself in the midst of our estrangement, at once gathering sinful man into one Body with the Saviour, and opening up a new and living way into the Holiest. That movement gathered

In conclusion, then, the distinctive identity of Jesus of Nazareth as the promised Messiah transforms and creates the distinctive identity of the disciple, who now shares with the crucified, risen, and glorified Lord a distinctive mission to the world.[27]

This exposition of the Lucan narrative incites the affirmation that it is this unity of *Word* and *Sacrament* which forms the central, critical, and crucial influence on the transformation and maintenance of a distinctive Christian identity, as well as a distinctive form of both liturgy and mission. *Central* because it is in the breaking of bread that the true identity of Jesus as the Messiah (and therefore his "real presence") is crystallized, actualized, and revealed as the crucified and risen One (e.g., "See my hands and feet, that it is I myself!"). *Critical* because this event, together with the interpretation of the Scriptures "concerning Himself" as the fulfillment of all messianic expectation, forces the disciples to reconsider all former expectations of the promised Messiah and brings into question both the previously held conceptions of the Messiah's identity and the disciples' identity in relation to Jesus Messiah. And *crucial* because it is in the unity of *Word* and *Sacrament* that the true identity of Jesus Messiah and that of his disciples are held in the balance, which in turn determines the symmetry of *mission*.

It is certainly no accident that in the opening chapters of the book of Acts one discovers the following: "Every day they devoted themselves to meeting together in the temple complex, and broke bread from house to house" (2:26). For it was the breaking of bread in their homes that

---

intensity until it reached decisive enactment in the crucifixion and fulfillment in the resurrection and ascension. Throughout the whole life and mission of Christ, hypostatic union and reconciliation, incorporation and atonement, involved each other in redemption and new creation. It is in that mutual involution that the Church is grounded as the one Body of the one Lord." Torrance, *Conflict and Agreement in the Church*, 239, 240–41.

27. "The Church that partakes of Holy Communion seeks to be renewed in it as a fellowship of reconciliation, but for that very reason it must be prepared to act out that which it receives at the Holy Table, and to live the reconciled life refusing to allow the sinful divisions of the world to have any place in its life. The Church that nourishes its life on earth by feeding upon the Body and Blood of Christ must live out in its own bodily existence the union and communion in which it participates in Christ. Holy Communion by its own innermost nature and by its whole intention and purpose requires the Church to work hard to eliminate its division, to resolve to seek reconciliation with all from whom it is estranged. . . . It belongs to the function of the Church, then, to enter into history in the service of reconciliation, to live out its divine life in the midst of the world's divisiveness, and by living as well as witnessing, to bring men into the fellowship of healing and peace with God." Torrance, *Conflict and Agreement in the Church*, 118–19.

determined the distinctive nature of their worship and identity as followers of Jesus Christ:

> It is especially characteristic of the "breaking of bread" . . . [that] in this meal there takes place an impressive anticipation of Christ's "coming"—or more accurately, his "return"—which he had promised. True, he will return to earth only at the end, but he also comes already now in his Church gathered to break bread. He has promised, "Where two or three are gathered in my name, there I am in the midst of them" (Matt. 18:20). This relationship between the early Church's eucharist and eschatology also corresponds perfectly to the meaning Jesus himself gave the act of distributing bread and wine at the Last Supper with his disciples . . . both elements were so intimately related that in the experience of Christ's presence in worship they really experienced in anticipation his final return . . . the early Church not only waited for "eschatological realization," but already experienced it—precisely in the eucharistic meals.[28]

Luke's narrative serves a liturgical purpose; that is, it discloses the distinctive nature of Christian worship in both form and content as the union of *Word* ("spoken/proclaimed") and *Sacrament* (the "visible" *Word*). This particular form of Christian worship enhances the revelation of the full and proper (i.e., the "distinctive" or true) identity of Jesus of Nazareth as the crucified and risen Messiah, and therefore his *real presence* in, with, and for the gathered community of disciples. The result of this encounter with Jesus Messiah in and through this particular liturgical form is the transformation and maintenance of the identity of the disciple(s) (i.e., the formation of a "distinctive" identity).

Following the contour of my contention, "the presence of Christ in the Eucharist is not confined to the consecrated elements of bread and wine. Christ is present, first, in the community which has assembled for worship; in the breaking of the bread and pouring-out of the cup; [and] he is present in the biblical word which is proclaimed."[29] Therefore:

> The Church at Eucharist is a structured community listening to the word of God, a community in continuity with the preaching, ministry, death and resurrection of its Lord, a community looking forward to the coming of the Kingdom, a community conscious

28. Cullmann, *Christology of the New Testament*, 211–12.

29. McBrien, *Catholicism*, 2:235.

of its sinfulness and repentant of its sins, a community convinced of the power of God's grace, a community ready to serve others, i.e. to carry out "the breaking of bread" beyond the Church, and a community here and now open to the presence of the Lord and his Spirit. "Only a person who is prepared in principle to entrust himself to the whole activity of the Church that takes place in the eucharist . . . will share even in the blessings and graces of this sacrament for the individual. . . . For ultimately these are nothing but that deeper and deeper union with the Church, her action and lot."[30]

30. Ibid., 767–68.

THREE

Anamnesis and "Real Presence"

For I received from the Lord what I also passed on to you: On the night when He
was betrayed, the Lord Jesus took bread, gave thanks, broke it, and said,
"This is My body, which is for you. Do this in remembrance of Me."
In the same way, after supper He also took the cup and said, "This cup is the new
covenant established by My blood. Do this, as often as you drink it, in remembrance of Me." For as often as you eat this bread and drink the cup,
you proclaim the Lord's death until He comes.

1 COR 11:23–26

THIS CHAPTER IS DEVOTED primarily to an exploration of the biblical,
theological, and liturgical meanings of the term *anamnesis*. What are
the connotations implicit in this concept? If *anamnesis* is a form of "remembrance," what is to be "remembered"—an event of the past, a personal
identity, a significant occurrence in the history of the religious community?
What does the term *anamnesis* imply in reference to the proposed liturgy
of *Word* and *Sacrament*?

A second objective of this chapter is to relate the concept of *anamnesis*
to the sacramental notion of "real presence"[1]—in particular, what is meant

1. In the proposed eucharistic-evangel, the term *real presence* refers primarily to the
pneumatic presence of Jesus Christ—though not to be identified (simply) with a localized
presence (e.g., in the elements, in the words of institution, etc.). In a previous chapter we
have already stated our belief that the use of the eucharistic concept of "transelementation" would advance ecumenical efforts with intercommunion and presents no serious
theological issues for most liturgical and sacramental traditions. Borrowing a familiar
phrase from the Lutheran confession, I affirm the presence of Christ to be "under, with,

by "real presence" in the liturgy of *Word* and *Sacrament*. What is the exact form and content of the implied disclosure: Where (according to biblical and theological standards) is this *real presence* located in the liturgical celebration, that is, in the sacred elements of bread and wine, in the words of institution, in the *epiclesis*,[2] in the gathered assembly, or in a combination of these liturgical components?

A third and final objective will be to investigate the relationship between *anamnesis, real presence,* and the *proclamation of the Word.* I have already argued that the manner in which Jesus of Nazareth fulfilled the Scriptures as the promised Messiah is to be perceived in a holistic pattern of interpretation.[3] Therefore, the proclamation of the Word includes

---

and in" the eucharistic celebration, but only in the following sense: (1) "under" the power of the Holy Spirit; (2) "with" the proclamation of the Word (in the forms delineated by "open-telling") and the enactment of the Sacrament; and (3) "in" the unity of the gathered assembly and the transformation of identity in conformation to the "image of Christ." The pneumatic presence of Christ includes the fullness of his identity (incarnation, ministry, death, resurrection, ascension, exaltation, reign, and return). There is, ultimately, only one "real presence" of Christ—although this presence may come about in various forms. Having said that, the Eucharist itself (bread broken and shared, cup poured out and shared) is to be acknowledged as a specific sacramental form of the Lord who is already personally (and really) present to/for the individual believer and community. The eucharistic celebration involves reciprocity—Christ's pneumatic "real presence" to/for the Church and the Church's "real presence" (in/with Christ) to and for God and in service to God's coming reign.

2. "Theologically, the epiclesis is rich and many faceted. First of all it serves as a reminder of the vital role of the Holy Spirit in the realization of the eucharist. The same Spirit who penetrated Jesus of Nazareth—now the risen, Spirit-filled Lord—is in the process of bringing Christ's work to fulfillment. This Spirit makes the body and blood of Christ, in a sense, capable of achieving its saving effects in the faithful . . . By making possible the presence of Christ offering himself *and* the acceptance of the assembled faithful, the Holy Spirit enables the full sacramental encounter to take place . . . drawing us into a new life. In addition, the epiclesis can serve as a reminder that God realizes the eucharist *for* the assembly, and in particular for the partaking assembly. . . . This underlines the unity between the transformation of the gifts ('consecration') and the transformation of the communicating assembly ('communion'). . . . The epiclesis also brings out the fact that God realizes the eucharist *through* the believing assembly. That it is God who takes the initiative, that God remains absolutely free and sovereign in realizing the eucharist, is undeniable . . . In the epiclesis the assembly, having recalled the events of saving history and having made thankful acknowledgment of these events, confesses its own helplessness. . . . The assembly appeals to God to transform both the gifts and the communicants so that this celebration of the eucharist may bring about a mutual eucharistic presence." Komonchak, Collins, and Lane, *New Dictionary of Theology,* 324–25.

3. My use of the term *holistic* parallels Luther's observation and contention that Holy Scripture is the cradle bearing the Christ. The primary function (from a Christian point

an *open-telling* of the narrative of redemptive history. Furthermore, we will explore the connections between the "spoken Word" and the "visible Word" in the liturgy of *Word* and *Sacrament*. In chapter 4, I analyze the relationship between *anamnesis, real presence*, the open-telling[4] of the narrative of redemptive history, and the transformation and maintenance of a distinctive Christian identity.

I contend that (1) *anamnesis* is more than the "remembrance" of an event of the past and more than the actualization of that past event in the present; rather, *anamnesis* includes the actualization of the *real presence* of Jesus of Nazareth as the crucified, risen, exalted, returning Messiah of God. *Anamnesis* is therefore the actualization of the One who was the power and saving presence in and through those historical events forming the pattern of the narrative of redemptive history, with the climax being the life, death, resurrection, and promised return of this same Jesus Messiah. (2) That the proclamation of the Word in the liturgy of *Word* and *Sacrament* includes the open-telling of the narrative of redemptive history with the narrative of the Christ-event forming the climactic center and therefore the fulfillment of this same narrative. (3) That such open-telling will also and at the same time serve to disclose the *real presence* of the triune God of love (whose center is Christ) and thereby enrich and enhance the trinitarian characterization of the eucharistic-evangel. And thus (4) *anamnesis* and the *real presence* disclosed (through the open-telling of the Christian story of

of view!) of the OT Scriptures is to bear witness to the Christ of God (Luke 1:68–79; 24:25–27; John 5:39; Acts 3:18–26; 18:28; Rom 1:2, et al.). The OT teaches that the Christ should come and these Scriptures are to be read in light of the crucified and risen Jesus of Nazareth. This is the meaning of Luke 24:13–35 (as paradigmatic); the events of the OT Scriptures no less than the words are the preparation for and foreshadowing of God's great act in the redemption of the world by the life, death, and resurrection of the Messiah. The OT Scriptures must be understood in light of this fulfillment in Jesus Christ, and the identity of Jesus Christ encloses the fullness of the OT Scriptures.

4. In the broad sense this term refers to those elements of the liturgy which include the reading of Scriptures, the prayers of thanksgiving, prayers of intercession, the hymns, responsive readings, etc., as these reflect the proclamation of God's eternal plan of salvation. Preaching (as essential to open-telling) is that form of proclamation which addresses the individual believer and community of faith in a particular setting and in a particular religious situation-in-life. In preaching God attaches an efficacious grace to the event and this grace is the divine self-communication, securing both the truth of the proclamation and the gift of hearing in/with faith. To this extent preaching is connected with the Word of God as witness, though not simply equated with the Word. Unlike the other mediums of open-telling, preaching involves (basically) three fundamental components: exegesis, interpretation, and application; all three are sustained and used by God in the power of the Holy Spirit.

redemption in union with the sacramental actions) will make possible the transformation of identity.

It is this fundamental relationship between *anamnesis, real presence*, and the open-telling of the narrative of redemptive history which makes the service of *Word* and *Sacrament* the most significant liturgical format contributing to the ongoing process of the transformation and maintenance of a distinctive Christian identity.[5] Throughout this essay the term *anamnesis* indicates more than the subjective representation of a particular event, or series of events, as an act of the "remembering" mind. The term signifies, first and foremost, a liturgical event which is the reactualization of the salvific action(s) of God and the presence of God (e.g., in the Passover Seder) as the personal force behind such action(s). Stated in more precise terms, in relation to the eucharistic-evangel the term implies the reactualization of the salvific action(s) of Jesus Christ and the "real [*pneumatic*] presence" of Christ (1 Cor 10:16).

Both *Word* and *Sacrament* are essential to *anamnesis*,[6] disclosed (1) as the *real presence* of Christ to/for the gathered assembly and individual communicant, and (2) in the unity of Christians as the one body partaking of the one bread (1 Cor 10:17). In and through such *anamnesis* the history of Jesus—the crucified, risen, reigning, and returning one—continues in and through the Christian community and its several ministries as a present reality, which is the result of the presence and power of the Holy Spirit (proceeding from the Father and the Son). The historical reality of Jesus' salvific action(s) and the identity of Jesus as the Christ of God transforms the identity (and worldview) of both the individual and community of faith. The *anamnetic* experience actualizes the transformation, confession, and subsequent action(s) of the individual and community of faith

---

5. "Since the *anamnesis* of Christ is the very content of the preached Word as it is of the eucharistic meal, each reinforces the other. The celebration of the eucharist properly includes the proclamation of the Word. . . . As it is entirely the gift of God, the eucharist brings into the present age a new reality which transforms Christians into the image of Christ and therefore makes them his effective witnesses." World Council of Churches, *Baptism, Eucharist and Ministry*, 12, 15.

6. "Under the new covenant Word and Sacrament are also equally united. Communion with God implies obedience to His Word as well as the reception of the body and blood of Christ. Christian worship also unites Word and Sacrament as two parts of one whole: the ministry of the Word and the ministry of the Sacrament." Thurian, *Eucharistic Memorial*, 2:54–55.

in solidarity with a broken humanity, groaning creation, and in symmetry with the cause of God in Christ Jesus.[7]

K. H. Bartels denotes that words in the LXX having the Greek root *mnē-* "reveal several related meanings, e.g., to proclaim, celebrate, confess with praise and adoration, solemnize, believe, obey, even to *become converted* or to *turn about.*"[8] The liturgical and theological dimensions implicit are clear from the following observation:

> The existence of the people of Israel, their faith in Yahweh as their saviour and redeemer . . . obedience to him as sovereign and as Lord of history, their public worship—all these things are grounded in their experience of his gracious help in the past. Hence, at their festivals the people of God are publically called upon to remember, and *as they do so*, the same God who did such

7. In his explication of *anamnesis* as "memorial," Max Thurian discusses the way in which the liturgies of the East offer a much broader perspective than is often evident in the eucharistic celebrations of the West. His presentation of this Eastern rubric lends admirably to much richer understanding of *anamnesis* and one that is resonant with my intended use in which the whole of the history of God, from creation to consummation, is lifted up, or better, "memorialized." Thurian writes: "In the Eastern liturgies there is a complete historical sequence of events, relating to the creation and redemption, running throughout the anaphora or eucharistic prayer. Thus in the liturgy of St. James, of Syrian provenance, the preface makes remembrance of creation, both visible and invisible, and this leads up to the Sanctus. The Postsanctus declares the creation of man, the law, the incarnation, life of Christ, and leads up to the institution narrative. There follows the anamnesis of the passion, cross and death, of the burial, resurrection, ascension, session, return and judgment. Next there is the Epiclesis which is a kind of solemn memorial of the role of the Holy Spirit in the Eucharist, as throughout the whole economy of redemption—the law, the prophets, the New Testament, the baptism of Christ and Pentecost. In this way the memorial is presented as a vast canvas depicting the creation and redemption, throughout the whole eucharistic prayer, apart from the interruption for the Sanctus, sung by all creatures visible and invisible, and the institution narrative. The same sequence, although even more developed, can be seen in the anaphora of St. Basil, of which the preface is a great thanksgiving to the Trinity adored by all the angelic powers. Although it has an analogous pattern, the anaphora of St. Chrysostom is much shorter, but the eucharistic prayer of all these Eastern anaphoras is closely unified by the historical sequence of the memorial. These fixed prayers present the whole mystery of creation and redemption at every celebration." Thurian, *Eucharistic Memorial*, 2:38–39. I see no theological hindrance to the use of such a liturgical rubric in the eucharistic celebration under consideration, regardless of the historical and confessional background of the community gathered for *Word* and *Sacrament*. The holistic liturgical attention to the "acts of God" will only reinforce the essential unity of the Triune God while further enriching the liturgical environment for the proposed transformation of a distinctive identity based on the historical self-disclosure of God as Father, Son, and Holy Spirit.

8. Bartels, "Remember, Remembrance," 3:232–33.

great things for them in the past, speaks to them once again at the present.[9]

Bartels also describes the ethical dimension to *anamnesis* when he argues: "To remember (in the aforementioned sense of the term) means to serve [God], to adore him, to obey and follow him, to *recognize* him as Creator and Lord. . . . The phrase 'to remember God' can be a formula summing up a [person's] religious standing."[10] Both "as they do" and "recognize" have been italicized in the above quotations because they suggest a relationship between the experience of *anamnesis* and the disclosure of the identity of God as "Creator and Lord" (shorthand for the distinctive characteristic of God's identity!). Also provocative is the proposal that to "remember God" be considered a "formula summing up a [person's] religious standing," which intimates that liturgical *anamnesis* and the individual's identity are closely related phenomenon.[11]

In the theology of the Old Testament this experience of *anamnesis* therefore "forms a bridge which links (the people of Israel in each generation) with the God of the forefathers, not because of a Herculean act of self-projection, but because the events of the tradition possess a power which continues to meet Israel in her (present realities)."[12] A classic example of this concept is found in the recitation cited as belonging to the "first-fruits" offering as recorded in Deuteronomy 26 (vv. 1–11, in particular). In the Hebrew language two nouns are used antecedently of the Greek *anamnesis*: "zikkaron ('memorial sign') and zeker ('remembrance/commemoration')."[13] The former term is associated primarily with the *covenant*, so that: "Signs and memorials serve within the (covenant) of grace both to guarantee and

9. Ibid., 3:332.

10. Ibid., 3:333.

11. "Liturgical anamnesis, therefore, is not mere mental recall of something past, over and done with, nor is it the fond recollection of something or someone absent. Rather, in the church's liturgical anamnesis before God, Christ is truly present now. Anamnesis in this sense has no adequate English equivalent; 'remembrance' or 'calling to mind' may translate the word but cannot do justice to the reality . . . the events of Jesus' life exist now in the risen Christ and are present in Christ in the liturgical remembrance. The events themselves must ever be recalled before God in worship for they reveal who Christ is for us and offer us his death and resurrection as the pattern which brings grace and salvation to the pivotal moments and to the whole of our lives in him." Komonchak, Collins, and Lane, *New Dictionary of Theology*, 17.

12. Bartels, "Remember, Remembrance," 3:236.

13. Ibid., 236–37.

maintain for each generation this eternal relationship. The cultic acts of Israel continually remind God of this eternal covenantal order. The cultic objects and rites act to guarantee that the covenant is not forgotten (by the community as well)."[14] The theological significance of the concept of "reminding" God is not unfamiliar to the formal literature of the Old Testament; for example, one is reminded of the covenant made between God and Noah (Gen 9:12–17!); others could be cited as well. As relates to the proposal under consideration, what is crucial to observe is the coupling of remembrance-recognition-covenant-obedience-presence of God and both liturgical and ethical actions taken. B. S. Childs argues that the redemptive history of Israel has a transcendent character; it represents events that are unique to a given time and place and yet are not bound to any temporal or spatial dimension. Remembrance, Childs writes,

> means more than that the influence of a past event (continues) to be felt in successive generations. . . . Rather, there was an immediate encounter, an actual participation in the great acts of redemption. . . . Actualization is the process by which a past event is contemporized for a generation removed in time and space from the original event. When later Israel responded to the continuing imperative of her tradition through memory, that moment in historical time likewise became an Exodus experience. Not in the sense that later Israel again crossed the Red Sea. . . . Rather, Israel entered the same redemptive reality of the Exodus generation.[15]

While I agree with the premise in the above comment, I would recommend that the *anamnesis* of the eucharistic-evangel be understood to actualize *both* the past salvific actions and the *real presence* of Christ, and under the power of the Holy Spirit as the God who is ever faithful and steadfast in/to his promises, people, and covenant (Christ did say, "This is My blood that establishes the *covenant*"). As crucial as it is, it is not the redemptive event *only* which enters the present realities of the worshipping community, but equally the God of redemption who is present to/for his people; it is not *merely* the recognition of the contemporary significance of some past redemptive event, but just as importantly, the redemptive *encounter* with the very same God who was the vital force active in that historical event of redemption and grace. To "enter the same redemptive reality" actually means encountering the same redemptive presence; this

14. Ibid., 237.
15. Ibid., 238.

encounter with the God of the exodus (more broadly stated, the Triune God of redemptive history), as active now, redeems and transforms the temporal and personal realities as well as identities of both worshipper and worshipping community.

Now, before considering the New Testament usage(s) of *anamnesis*, we must focus our attention on the Jewish Passover meal as the apparent antecedent to the Passover Jesus shared with his disciples "on the night when He was betrayed," and therefore the historical precedent for the whole of the eucharistic-evangel under consideration.[16]

At the heart of the Passover meal stands the great redemptive event of Israel's deliverance and freedom from the hard labor, oppression, and bondage the Hebrews had known in the land of Egypt. It is also said to be "the Passover sacrifice to the LORD, for He passed over the houses of the Israelites in Egypt when He struck the Egyptians and spared our homes" (Exod 12:27). The material elements (what could be called the "visible" word) of the meal include lamb, unleavened bread, bitter herbs, and wine; these elements bear the following symbolic significance: the lamb = sacrifice, the unleavened bread = the bread of affliction, the bitter herbs = the hard labor and bondage of Egypt, and the wine = the joy and festivity of deliverance. Just as central to the Passover meal (as event) is the recitation of the narrative of redemption (what could be called the "spoken" word), which apparently gave the meal its theological and liturgical character.[17] The

16. The relationship between the meal Jesus shared with his disciples and the Jewish Passover has not been consistently embraced as historically verifiable; however, as Alasdair Heron writes, "In the last thirty years, the opinion that the Last Supper was indeed a Passover meal has come once more to be widely held, chiefly because of the exceedingly full and detailed study of the evidence by Jeremias" (a reference to the now classic work titled *The Eucharistic Words of Jesus*). "While a certain uncertainty must remain, this makes it worthwhile to look at the Passover itself, and see what the shape of the Last Supper as a Passover might have been. Even if, after all, it was not a Passover, it nevertheless took place under the shadow of the approaching feast, and can properly be set against that background. Either way, the Passover ritual and its meaning can cast a good deal of light upon the Supper itself." Heron, *Table and Tradition*, 17–18.

17. "The significance for Jews down through the centuries of this celebration, this 'memorial,' and this recounting of the story of the Exodus deserves to be underlined, for otherwise we may pass it by too easily. For the children of Israel, the Exodus was not merely an inspiring tale from the remote past. It was the story of how God had called them out of slavery, given them a land, and made them a chosen nation. It was thus the story of his love and his mercy, his faithfulness not only to their ancestors but also to them. The old history was the key to their own identity as God's people; it was to be told and re-told from one generation to another, not merely as hallowed tradition but as a statement of their calling and destiny. . . . The 'remembering' involved here is not merely

retelling of the great event of redemption was (and is to this day) prompted by a question from a child at table: "What does this ritual mean to you?" (Exod 12:26)—to which the father responds with a narrative retelling of the entire exodus event. Implicit is the essential liturgical (and theological!) connection between the elements (*zikkaron*) with their deep symbolism and the narrative of redemption (*zeker*) as memorial to the Lord God.[18]

One could infer from the above paragraph that the symbolic character of the elements would be less poignant if not for the addition of the narrative retelling; the retelling of the narrative receives visual impact and profundity in the symbolic elements and in the actions associated with both aspects of the Passover meal. Both the material and verbal symbols are of fundamental importance to the theological and liturgical integrity of the worshipful event: "The correlation between sign and saving event gave the Jewish Passover a 'sacramental structure' . . . [the] Hebrew terms zikkaron and zeker (which correspond to anamnesis and 'memorial') gave clear and conscious expression to [the] theology of a presence that was based on the fact that God in his eternity transcends the temporal sequence proper to the created order."[19] Thus the emphasis is not merely on the presence of a past historical occurrence, but also and perhaps more importantly on the gracious presence of the God of salvation whose saving grace was profoundly disclosed in the exodus from Egypt, made known once again and with such startling clarity to those engaged in the Passover meal itself.

That this Passover meal was (and continues to be) a "commemoration" of the exodus event is beyond question, but not *merely* as historical recollection; in and through the living tradition of this liturgical celebration,

---

a matter of looking back to a past which is remote and distant. It is rather a setting of the present in the light of the past, a drawing of the two together in a way which transforms the present and renews hope for the future." Heron, *Table and Tradition*, 19–20.

18. "Two points in particular, both emphasized by Jeremias, are of special importance. First is the fact that the Passover included the *haggadah*, the interpretation of the meal and its components. This supplies a very likely setting for Jesus' reinterpretation of the bread and wine with which the main course opened and closed. Such a reinterpretation can hardly have been a normal or usual occurrence, but it would be much more comprehensible if it followed his giving the *haggadah* and explaining the meaning of the Passover itself. Second, the Passover itself as an act of remembrance, a *zikkaron*, offers a context in which the command, 'Do this for my remembrance,' can be seen as a natural extension and development of the Passover ritual. It also suggests what kind of 'remembering' Jesus had in mind. It was not to be a mere looking back to his death, but a celebration of his offering of himself which would continually recall his own to their allegiance to him, and to the deliverance he has secured for them." Heron, *Table and Tradition*, 22.

19. Emminghaus, *Eucharist*, 19.

present Israel encounters the very same God. It can therefore be asserted that the Passover:

> Meant . . . that the abiding fidelity of God to the covenant became present . . . [the] saving act which God performed in the historical past thus became in the Passover feast an abidingly present, gracious reality . . . it is the living God, Yahweh, who is ever present . . . reflection on the past serves to remind the believing Israelite that Yahweh can be counted upon to remain true. In this respect, the appeal to memory has a double function: it serves as a basis of appeal to Yahweh . . . and as such it also serves to encourage the believing Israelite that, however black his present predicament may be, he can still count on Yahweh. . . . When the Jew of today ends his Passover feast with the words, "Speedily lead your redeemed people to Zion in joy. Next year in Jerusalem!" his intention corresponds to Paul's when the latter tells the Christian that in the Eucharist "you proclaim the Lord's death until he comes" (1 Cor 11:26).[20]

The closing sentences of the above observation allude to the *eschatological* dimension of the Passover meal; within the context of this liturgical event, there is a fusion of time: past, present, and future are brought into a tensed modality. The *anamnetic* character of the Passover meal and the suggested fusion of time coalesce in what can only be called the *eschatological* dimension of the eucharistic-evangel: "As a matter of fact, our Christian theology of the sacraments is . . . grounded in the last analysis on (these concepts) already familiar to Judaism. . . . Against this background of the sacramental conception of the Passover which Jesus' contemporaries had, and of the symbolic character of the lamb, the bread, and the wine, Christ's action at the Last Supper becomes clear and intelligible."[21]

---

20. Ibid., 18–19; see also Bartels, "Remember, Remembrance," 3:238.

21. Emminghaus, *Eucharist*, 19. Thurian contends: "This eschatological perspective is an integral part of the Eucharist. At the Eucharist Christ appoints a kingdom unto the Church, which participates in it in advance, and in that communion with God which it involves; the Church already sits at table with Christ to eat and drink with Him and enter into communion with Him as in the Kingdom. As through the Eucharist they participate in this communion of the Kingdom and are admitted to the table of Christ, the faithful are assured of their entrance into the Kingdom of God at the Last Day that they may enjoy eternal communion with the Lord. Thus they receive the sign of their belonging to the coming Kingdom at the Eucharist; they are given the pledge that they will be able to enter in and have the right to sit at Christ's table 'to eat and drink' with Him in eternity." Thurian, *Eucharistic Memorial*, 2:66–67.

The following quote from A. G. Herbert clearly illustrates the profound nature of *anamnesis* in the eucharistic-evangel: "When Jesus said, 'Do this in remembrance of me' . . . he was assuredly not planning merely to keep before the disciples' minds that which they could anyhow never forget; it was to be a 'concrete remembering,' a bringing back out of the past into the present—of what? Not of sins, for by his Sacrifice they are taken away. But of the Sacrifice itself, or rather of *him*, crucified, risen from the dead, victorious through death."[22] There are two aspects of Herbert's observation deserving our attention: (1) that *anamnesis* is not an emotional and spiritual regression into the past, it is not the effort to get back there; and (2) that which is actualized in the present is not *merely* a past historical event, but the person of the Messiah, "*him*, crucified, risen from the dead, victorious through death" (see 1 Cor 15:3–4!). Herbert goes on to assert that "[as] Jesus at the Last Supper, taking his bread and wine, identified them with his Body and Blood, as the liturgical emblems of his Sacrifice; so [the disciples/Church], afterwards, taking *their* bread and wine, would do with them what he had done 'in objective remembrance of him.' Then he, in the power of his accepted Sacrifice, would be present in their midst in living power. Such would be his *anamnesis*."[23] Thus, in the bread broken and shared and the cup poured out and distributed, together with the open-telling of the redemptive event, the distinctive identity of Jesus Messiah is revealed as *real presence*.[24]

22. Herbert, *Theological Word Book of the Bible*, 143.

23. Ibid.

24. Once again Max Thurian provides clarification of the term *real presence* in a profoundly helpful observation: "The real presence of His body and blood is the presence of Christ crucified and glorified, here and now, under concrete signs. The meaning of every corporal presence is to attest concretely the presence of that person that he may enter into a concrete communion. By the real presence of His body and blood, the Church knows that Christ is there concretely in the midst and it receives Him by means of a concrete sign. The substantial presence of Christ does not denote a material presence, in the natural sense, but the presence of the profound reality of the body and blood of Christ crucified and glorified. . . . The real presence of Christ is not to be understood as localization limited to the elements of bread and wine; Christ cannot be shut up within the limits of the created world. But the bread and the wine at the Eucharist do become the privileged place where Christ Himself, in His humanity and deity, may be met and received. Christ glorified, by His power to subject all things, acts through the Holy Spirit and by His Word on the bread and wine, to make them into a place where the Church may meet Him and receive Him corporally, so that they are the instrument through which the Church can reach Him in the fullness of His humanity and deity." Thurian, *Eucharistic Memorial*, 2:121.

The consummate theologian Hans W. Frei, in his book *The Identity of Jesus Christ*, argues that the self-manifestation of an individual is based upon the presupposition of identity as the union of *intention-action*. The primary focus of Frei's work is on the resurrection of Jesus Christ as the *locus* of his identity as the *crucified living One*. It is the resurrection, as God's vindication of both Christ's intentions and actions (including Calvary as the point of Christ's ultimate obedience to the Father), which discloses Jesus' true identity as the promised Messiah of Israel. The full and proper identification of Jesus Messiah must be as the *crucified and risen One*; moreover, the recognition of Jesus' self-manifestation (post-resurrection, which would obviously include those "resurrection appearances" as recorded in the gospel accounts) presupposes such identification.

The Eucharist, as the *anamnesis* of this One's true identity, implies recognition of the *real presence* of the *crucified and risen* Christ. The *real presence* of Jesus Messiah is the self-manifestation of the One whose *intention-action* unity is disclosed in the breaking of bread and pouring out of the cup.[25] Therefore the modification to the Passover meal which Jesus shared with his disciples "on the night when He was betrayed" was a pre-passion self-disclosure of his true Messianic identity, which received its significance and meaning as a disclosure event only after the historical occurrences of Good Friday and Easter morning. Whenever the so-called primitive Church celebrated the Eucharist, this union of *intention-action* was once again actualized and the *real presence* disclosed.[26]

Notice the phrase "into a place where the Church may meet Him and receive Him." The biblical witness to any (almost all) encounters with Jesus Christ—and in particular where He was "received" (recall, for example, the story of Zacchaeus in Luke 19:2–9!)—eventuate in some form of conversion if not transformation of the individual encountering Christ. While there are exceptions to every rule, it is doubtful that most who encounter the risen, living, glorified Christ would come away from such an encounter without effect, but there is sufficient evidence in the experience of any seasoned pastor to warrant the contention that "reception" of Christ is absolutely essential to any conversional or transformational process! If we are considering an identity otherwise foreign to one's sense of self, it only stands to reason that the individual must be "receptive" to *both* the One whose identity is source and substance of that same transformational process and to the content of the identity assumed; Christ will not "force" such intense identification on anyone who is less than "receptive" to his open invitation (see, in particular, John 14:23!).

25. "Christ instituted the eucharist as a memorial (*anamnesis*) of his whole life and above all of his cross and resurrection. Christ, with everything he has accomplished for us and for all creation, is present himself in this memorial, which is also a foretaste of his kingdom." Clifford, *For the Communion of the Churches*, 14.

26. Frei, *Identity of Jesus Christ*, 17–34, esp. 18–20.

Hans Frei proposes that the identity of Jesus Christ is disclosed in the union of sacramental action(s) and narrative retelling of his life, death, and resurrection; both action(s) and retelling are necessary to a comprehensive identification (the true identity as *real presence* of Christ), as both intention and action(s) are necessary constituents of identity formation and self-manifestation. In reference to my proposal in this essay, the following observation of Frei is pertinent:

> It is . . . notorious that ecclesiastical bodies characterized by sacramental or Biblical traditionalism have found passionate commitment to the fulfillment of human hopes and aspirations in history a difficult thing. On the other hand, Christian moral activities, trying hard to bestow significance on Sacraments and Biblical Word in the compass of a passionate concern for the world, have had equally great difficulty becoming convinced of—and doing justice to—the integrity of Word and Sacrament—the two permanent or localized expressions of Christ's identity and presence. . . . It is only by reference . . . to the complete unity of Jesus Christ's identity and presence given to us now . . . that Word and Sacrament cohere with passionate Christian concern for the world. . . . The church is founded on and sets forth the unity of both only through the presence of Jesus Christ.[27]

The theologian Peter Hodgson makes a similar claim when he contends that "there can be no recognition, and hence no presence, of the risen Jesus apart from the memory of the historical Jesus. . . . For us . . . this is of necessity mediated by the traditions concerning his historical word and deed. Without these traditions there would be no means of recognizing *who* is now present; in this sense, the risen Jesus is "identified" by reference to the historical Jesus."[28]

I would merely add that the open-telling of redemptive history, as the interpretation and proclamation of the Scriptures fulfilled in Jesus of Nazareth as the promised Messiah, further enhances the worshipper's recognition of the full (true) identity of Jesus as the Christ of God now present in the sacramental meal. While Hodgon's use of "memory" does not parallel my broader definition of *anamnesis*, his concern bears decisively on my own when he asserts that the knowledge of the "traditions concerning

---

27. Ibid., 158.

28. *Jesus—Word and Presence*, 269–70.

[Jesus'] historical word and deed" enhances the recognition of "*who* is now present."

Although one cannot arrive at a scholarly consensus regarding the antecedent to the Last Supper, that is to say, whether it was in fact the Passover meal of traditional Jewish practice that Jesus shared with his disciples on that final night, it can be stated that "it had the same basic structure: the words over the bread, its breaking and sharing; the words over the wine, and its sharing."[29] However, that Jesus identified the bread and wine with his own body and blood is beyond denial. Therefore it must be noted that "there is an undeniable continuity between what happened at the Last Supper and what the disciples did together at meals after the resurrection."[30] In an extended discussion of what one can postulate as the antecedent ritual to the Lord's Supper, the theologian T. F. Torrance writes:

> The origins of the Lord's Supper evidently lie in the Passover Meal, to which there has already been assimilated the Covenant Meal with its cup of wine. The original Passover according to the records in Exodus is rather different, for example, from the Passover celebration that we find to-day in the Jewish *Passover Haggadah*. The latter has of course developments in detail that may or may not be legitimate extensions of the original rite, but the essential pattern found in the *Passover Haggadah* is clearly one in which the original elements of "the Passover of Egypt" (as it was called in Judaism) have been enlarged and somewhat transformed by assimilation to the Covenant Meal of the Israelites at Mount Sinai, which took account of the mighty events of Israel's redemption that transpired after the celebration of the first Passover. There was added to the Passover Meal the consumption of wine, for it was a joyful and thankful feast before the presence of God, and this was called "the Passover of the Generations." It would appear that the *Kiddush* with its rite of sanctification using a cup of wine and water, observed at the beginning of the festivals, also reflects a similar tradition, so that its influence upon the Last Supper must also be taken into account.[31]

As fascinating as is this discussion of what might have been the relationship between the meal Jesus shared with his disciples on that last night and the traditional Passover meal, our concern is equally to demonstrate

29. McBrien, *Catholicism*, 2:758.

30. Ibid., 2:759.

31. Torrance, *Conflict and Agreement in the Church*, 2:134.

the relationship between the meal Jesus shared on the night he was betrayed and the proposed liturgy of the eucharistic-evangel. On just this issue Torrance offers this wonderful commentary:

> The resurrection inevitably modified the character of the meal, as it was intended to do, so that the Lord's Supper as celebrated in the Church was not just the prolongation of the Last Supper (when did this expression *Last Supper* arise?) but was a "sacramental" continuation of the acts of Christ in the miraculous feeding of the multitudes (as with manna) and entailed the "sacramental" extension into the Church of the resurrection meals of the risen Lord with His disciples. The relation of the Lord's Supper as celebrated in the Church to the Last Supper as celebrated on the night in which He was betrayed is, therefore, not unlike the relation between "the Passover of Egypt" and "the Passover of the Generations." Thus, in distinction from the Last Supper, the Lord's Supper enshrines both the historical Supper before the crucifixion of Jesus and a celebration of the resurrection. The Lord's Supper is a historical action in remembrance of Christ, after the fashion of the Last Supper, and a Messianic Meal with the risen Lord, joined together in one. That conjunction also affects the meaning of *anamnesis* in the Supper.[32]

Johannes H. Emminghaus surveys the development of the Eucharist as a liturgical practice in early Christian communities, concluding that in the earliest stages of such expansion, the Eucharist was celebrated as part of a general communal meal (*agape*), which only gradually evolved as an isolated liturgical practice.[33] With such a truncated practice "what had been eliminated was not simply the sociableness of the agape, but the leisure for proclamation, reading, exhortation, explanation, song, etc. as well."[34] Emminghaus theorizes that "in order to restore such basic elements of a Christian liturgy as reading, singing, preaching, and praying, a liturgy of the word was added to the Eucharist. A model for this was ready at hand in the liturgy of the synagogue."[35] These conclusions reached by Emminghaus are central to my contention that the eucharistic-evangel, as the liturgy of *Word* and *Sacrament*, entails the overall interrelatedness of the *spoken Word* and the *visible Word*; and it was necessary to recapture this unity so as to regain the fullest expression of this liturgical event. Though some

---

32. Ibid., 2:136.
33. Emminghaus, *Eucharist*, 23–31.
34. Ibid., 30.
35. Ibid., 31.

may contend the following affirmation to be nothing short of hyperbole, the comment speaks forcefully to the necessity for maintaining the unity of *Word* and *Sacrament*: "The fact that Word and sacraments imply each other forbids us either to set one against the other or to assert the primacy of either over the other."[36] The unity of the *spoken Word* and *visible Word* in the development of the eucharistic-evangel helps maintain "the dialogical structure proper to all liturgy."[37]

This "dialogical structure" emerges in the following pattern:

> God initiates the process of salvation and addresses himself to [humankind]. His word reaches [persons] and summons them to faith; through listening, silence, or hymnic reflection on the great God, the word that is heard creates a place for itself in the hearer, and the proclamation by the preacher, as [he/she] actualizes the word or gives it relevance here and now, makes it easier for the word to make its way into the soul. Finally, [persons] turn back to God in faith, confession, and shared prayer.[38]

This "dialogical structure" (as has already been argued in chapter 1) is an essential stimulus in the transformation of identity. I would also call attention to the phrase "God initiates the process of salvation," which lends further credibility to my contention that God (in Christ and under the empowerment of the Holy Spirit) takes the initiative in the *transformational process* itself. The one whose true identity is disclosed as *real presence* is the power behind the transformation of both individual and communal identities. In relation to the latter (i.e., communal), it is evident that in so much of the contemporary Church the theological conceptualization of Church as the "Body of Christ" has been lost on many Christian believers, who tend to view the Church more in terms of a voluntary organization, or in even more secular terms, an institution comparable to any other "business"! The point being that the need for a genuine "identity transformation" is not restricted to the individual believer alone, but is just as critical to the nature of the Christian community, and in particular in a context in which

---

36. Clifford, *For the Communion of the Churches*, 84. In equally poignant terms, T. F. Torrance writes: ". . . it is the Word which sacramentalizes, and apart from the Word sacraments cannot exist. Apart from the Word there is only an empty sign that is nothing but a ceremony. *Kerygma* and sign go together and cannot be sundered. In *kerygma* the Word is made flesh. In the sacraments the Word is made *flesh*." Torrance, *Conflict and Agreement in the Church*, 2:164–65.

37. Emminghaus, *Eucharist*, 34.

38. Ibid.

so many believers have traded the feast of identity in Christ for the pottage of cultural identification.

In a fascinating account referenced in the *First Apology* of Justin Martyr (c. 138 AD), we are given a candid glimpse of this liturgical unity in his description of the Sunday liturgy:

> And on the day named after the sun, all who live in city or countryside assemble, and the memoirs of the apostles or writings of the prophets are read for as long as time allows. When the lector has finished, the president addresses us admonishing us and exhorting us to imitate the splendid things we have heard. Then we all stand and pray, and . . . when we have finished praying, bread, wine, and water are brought up. . . . The president offers prayers of thanksgiving . . . and the people give their assent with "Amen!" Next, the gifts over which the thanksgiving has been spoken are distributed, and each one shares in them, while they are also sent via the deacons to the absent believers.[39]

This second-century witness to Christian liturgical practice reflects themes also evident in the Lucan narrative of the Emmaus road encounter, for example, the specific texts shared and explicated, the gathering at table, the thanksgiving, the distribution of "the gifts." Also evident are the two characteristics of the eucharistic-evangel: (1) The *spoken Word*, represented by readings from the "memoirs of the apostles or the writings of the prophets," as well as the "address" of the "president;" and (2) the *visible Word*, represented by the "bread, wine, and water . . . distributed, and [in which] each one shares." Furthermore, the exhortation to "imitate the splendid things we have heard" is, I would contend, an injunction to have one's personal identity impacted by those same "splendid things" which have been heard. Therefore, "the word is ultimately effective . . . only if it creates a sense of community. . . . What is proclaimed must be lived (1 Cor 11:26)."[40]

Once again in the words of Peter Hodgson: "Jesus is present in terms not of a simple imitation of what he said and did, but of a responsible correspondence to his being as presence, a correspondence that comes to focus at three points: a new language, a new mode of existence, and a new *praxis*."[41] I couch this "new mode of existence" in terms of the transformation of

---

39. Ibid., 36.

40. McBrien, *Catholicism*, 2:760.

41. Hodgson, *Jesus—Word and Presence*, 276.

identity on individual and communal levels; in this fashion the "correspondence to [Jesus'] being as presence" is made manifest.

The *anamnesis* of the eucharistic-evangel is, therefore, a communion *in* Christ as well as *with* Christ; as an event *in* Christ it is to remember one's personal and temporal identity as united to/with that of Christ (crucified, risen, reigning, and returning) as the true presence disclosed in the liturgy of *Word* and *Sacrament*; as a communion *with* Christ it is to remember his true identity as the one who fulfills the Scriptures, an identity that is Alpha and Omega:

> The Lord's Supper establishes and celebrates the communion that exists not only between the Church and Christ but also within the Church—i.e., not only "with Christ" but also "in Christ." And it is a communion that looks always not only to the past—i.e., to the Last Supper and to the redemptive events that followed it—but also to the future, "until he comes" (1 Cor 11:26). . . . Christ's presence in the Eucharist, therefore, is the presence not only of the crucified and risen one, but also the presence of the one who is yet to come.[42]

With Hodgson we would conclude that "the Eucharist, therefore, is a meal of remembrance and thanksgiving, of fellowship, and of anticipation. It looks at once to the past, the present, and the future (a 'tensed modality'). . . . Through the Eucharist, the Church proclaims its faith in the Lordship of Jesus and in the coming of the kingdom . . . the Church manifests and more fully recognizes and deepens its unity in Christ (through a *transformation and maintenance of identity, individual and corporal*) . . . the Church sets the pattern for its own ministry to those in need" (the *praxis* giving evidence to an identity in symmetry with the "mission" of Jesus Messiah).[43]

Patterns of the *anamnetic character* in the liturgy of *Word* and *Sacrament* include the following: (1) It is the disclosure event of the triune God of love, whose central disclosure is Jesus Messiah as the *host* of this celebration; (2) the individual and community sharing a genuine and fruitful union "in and with Christ;" this union forming the bond which initiates and sustains the transformation of identity; (3) directing time backwards and forwards, symbolic of the "already" and "not yet" dimensions of both redemptive history and the process of transformation; and (4) a covenant meal and celebration which discloses both the presence and promises of

42. McBrien, *Catholicism*, 2:760.

43. Hodgson, *Jesus—Word and Presence*, 589.

God in Christ, in the present and for the future. In the liturgy of *Word* and *Sacrament*, "We are required only to keep our eyes and ears open for the family relationships between Jesus' words and deeds, his life and death, and our own experience of existence. . . . Jesus' life and death can disclose to us our own experience of existence and express it critically in such a way that we can recognize in it authentic possibilities for human life. To live like this is to have a good life. In that case there is a link between Jesus' life and ours."[44] With such an attitude or "mind" (see Phil 2:5!)[45] as this, we remain receptive to the disclosure event and to the ever present possibility of transformation of identity under the power of the Spirit of our crucified, risen, reigning, and returning Lord Christ—the true Messiah.

44. Schillebeeckx, *Interim Report on the Books Jesus and Christ*, 63.

45. The reader is directed to the most recent work of Evangelical scholar Mark A. Noll, *Jesus Christ and the Life of the Mind*, in which he argues cogently for the manner in which a "mind" transformed in Christ is capable of coming to a deeper comprehension of and appreciation for a wide variety of other intellectual pursuits—including all manner of academic study. What I find most intriguing about this profound piece of writing in terms of its potential relevance to my proposal is the manner in which the transformation of the "mind" in Christ makes possible an all-inclusive worldview, or better stated a worldview shaped, informed, and guided by Christ Jesus as Lord of the whole of the created order! My purpose is to encourage the Church catholic to embrace the richness of the fuller eucharistic-evangel as the vehicle for actualization of an inheritance that is beyond human capacity to imagine, bringing the glory of God in Christ into the realm of the Church's life, mission, and ministry of reconciliation.

FOUR

Anamnesis and the "Open-Telling" of Redemptive History

> The teaching of the apostles, the table fellowship, and the prayers transform the community of bread into a community of faith. The breaking of bread is an integral part of the whole liturgy of the Christian life. A separation of the eucharistic meal, whether conceptually or practically, from the preaching of the word, the teaching of the apostles, the prayers of the Church, and the companionship of the faithful, weakens the whole structure of the body.[1]

I N THIS CHAPTER WE turn our attention to an investigation of the relationship between the category of *anamnesis* and the open-telling (i.e., "proclamation" in the broadest sense of the term)[2] of the narrative of

---

1. Vondey, *People of Bread*, 228.

2. In the broadest sense of the term in my usage, *open-telling* refers to those elements of the liturgy which include the reading of Scriptures, the prayers of thanksgiving, prayers of intercession, the hymns, responsive readings, etc., as these reflect, resonate with, or better encapsulate the proclamation of God's eternal plan of salvation. Preaching (as the central act of open-telling) is that form of proclamation which addresses the individual believer and the community of faith gathered for worship in a particular religious situation or *Sitz im Leben*. In preaching God attaches an efficacious grace to the *event* and this grace, as divine self-communication, secures both the truth of the proclamation and the gift of hearing in/with faith. To this extent preaching is connected to the Word of God—though not to be equated with it in some simplistic way. Unlike the other mediums of open-telling, preaching involves three fundamental components: (1) exegesis, (2) interpretation, and (3) application; all three are sustained/used of God in the power of the Holy Spirit.

redemptive history as components essential to the eucharistic-evangel and instrumental in the transformative process. For this subject I refer, first, to *Baptism, Eucharist, and Ministry* (Faith and Order Paper 111), a publication of the World Council of Churches. This document states that "although the eucharist is one complete act, it will be considered here under the following aspects: thanksgiving to the Father, memorial of Christ, invocation of the Holy Spirit, communion of the faithful, meal of the Kingdom."[3] These "aspects" represent a holistic depiction of redemptive history; that is, the Trinitarian structure is expressive of a celebration that incorporates the entire pattern of redemptive history. In a provocative essay titled "Story and Eucharist," theologian S. W. Sykes explores the relationship between *anamnesis* in the Eucharist and the *theology of Christian story*.[4] Sykes employs the "aspects" from *Baptism, Eucharist, and Ministry* and correlates these with "four components in story grammar: a setting, a theme, a plot, and a resolution."[5]

When the components of "story grammar" are related to the pattern of redemptive history, the following format emerges: "(1) the setting = human history; (2) the theme = rescue from human destruction; (3) the plot = revelation and incarnation; and (4) the resolution = the eschatological dimension."[6] In more explicit terms, when the four components of "story grammar" are related to the four "aspects" as enunciated in *Baptism, Eucharist, and Ministry*, the following pattern is recommended: "(1) the setting = thanksgiving to the Father [for creation]; (2) the theme = memorial of the Son [redemption]; (3) the plot = communion of the faithful [the church in the power of the Holy Spirit]; and (4) the resolution = the meal of the Kingdom [eschatology]."[7] Particular attention should be given to number three in each case (i.e., "the plot = revelation and incarnation" and "the plot = communion of the faithful"); at the very least this correlation intimates the category of "real presence" as defined in an earlier chapter of this essay.[8]

The primary locus of Sykes' proposal is on the "category of sacrifice."[9] The point at which the proposal extended by Sykes contributes to my own

3. World Council of Churches, *Baptism, Eucharist, and Ministry*, 10.

4. Sykes, "Story and Eucharist," 365.

5. Ibid., 366.

6. Ibid., 367.

7. Ibid., 370.

8. See footnote 1 in chapter 3.

9. Sykes, "Story and Eucharist," 365.

is tellingly disclosed in the assertion that when one relates "the elements of story grammar to the themes of eucharistic theology . . . the category of anamnesis [is] by no means [to be] reserved to the work of Christ. [If] the Eucharist entails the open telling and thus recollection of the Christian story, then the setting, the plot, and the resolution are, along with the theme, constituent parts of the *anamnesis*."[10] Thus the "open telling" includes a more holistic and panoramic interpretation and proclamation of God's redemptive history—from the point of creation, through human (Adamic) estrangement due to sin, including the call of, promise to, and covenant with Abraham, the sojourn in Egypt, the drama of exodus, wilderness wandering and entrance into the promised land, leading up to and including the climactic fulfillment of redemptive history in the Christ-event, pressing into the open future of eschatological consummation (i.e., the return of Christ and the establishment of God's reign in all its fullness).

Past, present, and future are held together in a *tensed modality*; in this fashion time is not suspended, rather time is now gifted with a deeper purpose and meaningful direction. As the temporal and personal identity narrative of the worshipper (and worshipping community) is taken up into the broader, more panoramic narrative of God's redemptive history, a powerful transformation of identity ensues. Both forms of identity (personal and communal) are perceived as having a *new* meaning, purpose, content, and direction in the lineage of the saints of both Old and New Testaments. The climactic fulfillment of this proclamatory event is, no doubt, the "open telling" of the Christ-event. It is *this* narrative account which brings greater clarity and sharper focus to the identity of God in Christ:

> The love of God is forcefully portrayed in the beginning (Creation) as the divine vulnerability that risks the abuse of freedom by a covenant partner but patiently and stubbornly pursues a rebel creation (the story from the "Fall" of Adam to the coming of Christ). The power of God is reconceived in the light of the *central* chapter of the story in which "the weakness of God (proves) stronger than men" (in Christ) . . . the cross and resurrection and the liberation accomplished there goes forward in a manner commensurate with its instrument (the Church) . . . over the time line of long-suffering that reaches into the eschaton itself (the Kingdom).[11]

10. Ibid., 368.

11. Stoup, *Promise of Narrative Theology*, 352.

The similarities between the elements of "story grammar," the "open telling" of the narrative of redemptive history (as depicted in the above quotation), and the essential "aspects" of the eucharistic-evangel are readily apparent.

My intention is not to diminish the centrality of the Christ-event in the proposed liturgy of eucharistic-evangel; to do so would only threaten to diminish his central role in redemptive history as well! I am suggesting, however, that the proclamation (or *spoken Word*) and interpretation of redemptive history in a holistic pattern further enhances the identification ("recognition") of the *real presence* of Jesus Christ as the one who fulfills the Scriptures (i.e., the Law, Prophets, and Writings) and therefore his true identity; this model for proclamation correlates with the Lucan model found in the Emmaus road account, for example, "Then beginning with Moses and all the Prophets, He interpreted for them all the things concerning Himself in all the Scriptures" (Luke 24:27). The true identity of Jesus Messiah disclosed in the eucharistic-evangel includes all that preceded the "first Advent" and all that transpires to his "second Advent." As Alasdair Heron contends:

> His presence is not merely a continuation or extension of what he was two thousand years ago; it is his bearing upon our present to make it a form and means of *his* presence, opening it (and us) to his future. It is in the eschatological presence of the crucified and risen Christ that the main lines of the New Testament invite us to discern the significance of the Eucharist. What he was, suffered and did for us he makes ever and again contemporary in its completeness for us who are still *in via*. We have to do not only with present, but with past, present *and future* meeting in him,, and making him the ground, accompaniment *and goal* of our journey. He stands *before* us, not merely behind or with us.[12]

The relationship between the *spoken Word* and the *visible Word* in the liturgy of *Word* and *Sacrament* can only be properly understood as a necessary connection: "It is the Christian narrative which provides the proper and necessary context of the sacraments. . . . In themselves and by themselves the sacraments are meaningless. They receive meaning only when they are located in the larger context of the confessional narrative they presuppose."[13] This may, at first blush, appear to be hyperbole; but then we should recall both our exposition of the Lucan text and the conclusions

12. Heron, *Table and Tradition*, 153.
13. Stoup, *Promise of Narrative Theology*, 253.

reached by Emminghaus in his investigation into the early practice of the Eucharist. To actualize the Christian story of redemption implies a form of confession in and through which "the narrative identity of the self" is transformed by "the narrative history of God's redemptive activity" (the "central chapter" in the narrative of the Christ-event).[14] As George Stroup maintains in his book *The Promise of Narrative Theology: Recovering the Gospel in the Church*, "Revelation ('real presence') occurs when the Christian narrative collides with personal identity and the latter is reconstructed by means of the former . . . when that narrative becomes disclosive of the truth about personal and communal identity . . . [this disclosure becomes] the occasion for the transformation of personal identity . . . when the Spirit enables personal and communal identity to be fused to the narrative history of God's grace."[15]

The role of the Holy Spirit "is not to be correlated with one element of the Christian story recalled in the Eucharist but with the act of eucharistic anamnesis as such!"[16] Through the empowering presence of the Spirit, the eucharistic-evangel becomes "part of the divine story, woven into the very fabric of the worship of heaven and the communion of the Holy Trinity."[17] The Spirit-empowered character of the eucharistic-evangel (in its holistic pattern of *spoken Word* and *visible Word*) becomes paradigmatic of all worship "in spirit and in truth." To quote from *Baptism, Eucharist, and Ministry* (see, in particular, paragraphs 16–18):

> The whole action of the eucharist has an "epiklectic" character because it depends upon the work of the Holy Spirit. . . . The Church, as a community of the new covenant, confidently invokes the Spirit, in order that it may be sanctified and renewed, led into all justice, truth and unity, and empowered to fulfill its mission in the world. . . . The Holy Spirit through the eucharist gives a foretaste of the Kingdom of God; the Church receives the life of the new creation and the assurance of the Lord's return.[18]

Both the "epiklectic" and "anamnetic" characteristics of the liturgy of *Word* and *Sacrament* serve to transform and maintain a distinctive Christian identity on individual and communal levels of existence: "United to our

14. Ibid., 254f.

15. Ibid., 257–58.

16. Sykes, "Story and Eucharist," 371.

17. Ibid.

18. World Council of Churches, *Baptism, Eucharist, and Ministry*, 13.

Lord and in communion with all the saints and martyrs, we are renewed in the covenant sealed by the blood of Christ."[19] Certainly one implication of the proposal I am offering is clearly affirmed by paragraph 30 of *Baptism, Eucharist, and Ministry*, which reads: "Christian faith is deepened by the celebration of the Lord's Supper. Hence, the eucharist should be celebrated frequently."[20]

A second implication of my proposal for the liturgy of *Word* and *Sacrament* and in relation to the transformation and maintenance of a distinctive Christian identity is one that will be taken up in detail in the next chapter, and that is the role baptism and confirmation play in Christian identity formation. For the moment I would merely say that *if* these worshipful expressions were celebrated within the context of the liturgy of *Word* and *Sacrament*, the eucharistic-evangel would be appropriately perceived as the central locus of Christian identity, which begins with baptism and finds self-expression by confession in the event of confirmation.

A further implication is that the Eucharist itself is not to be perceived as *a* drama of salvation, enacted merely as a part of "eighth day" worship; the entire eucharistic-evangel (as the essential union of *spoken* and *visible* Word) is to be comprehended as *the* drama of salvation, the open-ended eschatological drama, in which the community of faith plays a significant role. This dramatic character of the eucharistic-evangel—as the "anamnesis" of redemptive history, with its fulfillment disclosed in Jesus Messiah, and as the "anamnesis" of the past salvific action as the personal force behind all sacramental action(s)—is also and at the same time the "anamnesis" of the divine identity—embracing the world in which the promise of renewal and transformation has been given: "The world is present in the thanksgiving to the Father, where the Church speaks on behalf of the whole creation; in the memorial of Christ, where the Church, united with its great High Priest and Intercessor, prays for the world; in the prayer for the gift of the Holy Spirit, where the Church asks for sanctification and new creation."[21]

The eucharistic-evangel (as the liturgical union of *Word* and *Sacrament*) "embraces all aspects of life . . . (including personal and communal identity) . . . and involves the believer in the central event of the world's history."[22] Moreover, it is in this liturgical event that the Church's identity as

19. Ibid., 12.
20. Ibid., 16.
21. Ibid., 14.
22. Ibid.

the "people of God" is fully disclosed.[23] In fact, "no Christian community can be built up unless it has its basis and center in the celebration of the most Holy Eucharist. . . . [and] . . . [i]f this celebration is to be sincere and thorough, it must lead to various works of charity and mutual help, as well as to missionary activity and to different forms of Christian witness."[24] Discerning the "body" means discerning the corporate nature of our Christian identity (1 Cor 11:12) as "the body of Christ" (1 Cor 12:27). The eucharistic-evangel discloses our identity in union with our Lord Christ (1 Cor 10:16).

Therefore we must discern our own (personal and corporate) identity in relation to Christ's proper (read: true) identity in such a manner that his mission to and for the world becomes our own: "The renewal in the Eucharist of the covenant between the Lord and (the community) draws the faithful into the compelling love of Christ and sets them afire. From the liturgy, therefore, and especially from the Eucharist, as from a fountain, grace is channeled into us; and the sanctification of [persons] in Christ and the glorification of God, to which all other activities of the Church are directed as toward their goal, are most powerfully achieved."[25] These words, gleaned from a document of Vatican II, represent in an insightful fashion the relationship between the liturgy of *Word* and *Sacrament* and the transformation and maintenance of a distinctive Christian identity and mission.

At this juncture I wish to share—other than for the reasons already stated—why it is I have chosen to focus on the Emmaus road account from the Gospel of St. Luke. Throughout the next several paragraphs I am deeply indebted to the insights of Emile Mersch, SJ.[26] One of the obvious characteristics of Luke's portion of the New Testament is the fact that he—unlike the other gospel writers—presents his narrative in two separate and yet related "books."[27] While my intention in this essay is very different from that of Emile Mersch, I have come to appreciate the manner in which he draws attention to Luke's theological brilliance in offering his gospel and sequel as two chapters of one whole narrative of redemption. I haven't made

---

23. Ibid.

24. Vatican Council II, *Documents of Vatican II*, 545–46.

25. Ibid., 142–43.

26. Mersch, *Whole Christ*, esp. 71–73.

27. Some have argued that the book of the Acts of the Apostles should have been placed immediately after St. Luke's Gospel; but I would trust (as do biblical scholars in general) that those who formulated our canon knew exactly what they were doing and why they separated these two pieces of writing (even though they are obviously connected).

use of the theological category of "Mystical Body" in this essay for fear that it would create unnecessary controversy and therefore distract from my purpose; it is, however, the term employed by Mersch and is, for obvious reasons, essential to his own proposal.

In his description of Luke's depiction of the "Mystical Body," he offers the following observation: "When taken alone, St. Luke's Gospel contains little of its own on the subject of the Mystical Body for the simple reason that it was not intended to be taken alone. The author himself describes it as a beginning, as 'a first account' (*protos logos*), to be explained and completed by a sequel or second account (*deuteros logos*), which is the Acts of the Apostles; that there is real continuity is attested by many indications in both parts of the complete work."[28]

Mersch goes on to suggest that the "purpose of the twofold work, as we know, is to show the universal character of the salvation brought by Christ. The Gospel lets us see this universality in its source, by showing how totally and how supernaturally human are these 'good tidings' and the Master who announces them; the Acts let us see it is its realization, by describing how these good tidings of salvation are carried to the whole world."[29] Yet, it is in the following comment that Mersch's interpretation of the twofold nature of Luke's narrative of the "Mystical Body" has direct bearing on my proposal:

> The distinctive note of St. Luke's account of the Mystical Body is its emphasis on the catholicity, the universality of that Body. It was left for the faithful companion of Paul to proclaim, in the language of actual facts, how in His Body, which is the Church, Christ is exactly what He is in Himself, in His Body of flesh: the mystical Christ, like the historical Christ, is destined for the whole world; His is a life universally human. The same Spirit who led the Saviour, in the days of His mortal life, to preach the Gospel to the poor, to the captives, to the blind, leads Him even now in the days of His mystical life in the Church, to take possession of, and to unite in Himself the poor human world that has wandered far from light and life.[30]

I would hope that any reader of this essay would not fail to hear resonance in this amazing piece of theological insight to the proposal at hand!

28. Mersch, *Whole Christ*, 71.
29. Ibid., 71–72.
30. Ibid., 72.

Before elaborating on these observations made by Mersch regarding the twofold nature of Luke's account and its "family resemblance" to my proposal and restrictive employment of Luke's Gospel, I would offer one more observation from Mersch. He also contends that where the "Gospel relates how the word of salvation starts out from Galilee and how, by way of Judea and Samaria, it comes to Jerusalem; the Acts tell how the same word goes forth from Jerusalem, passing through Judea and Samaria, to reach the ends of the earth. Hence the scene in Jerusalem, with which the Gospel closes, is not the end of the story; it is a turning point, a new beginning; the mortal life of Christ ends only to initiate the flow of His mystical life."[31] This observation also resonates most clearly with my contention that the Emmaus road narrative—as paradigmatic of the spiritual power of the prototypical eucharistic-evangel—empowers the formally forlorn and despondent disciples to initiate the issuance of the "good news" from within the city of Christ's crucifixion and death as prelude to its furtherance throughout the whole world!

I find it striking that Luke employs in two different literary settings (i.e., his Gospel and Acts) conversional experiences that happen to involve being "on the road"—one being the account of the road to Emmaus and the other the account of the Apostle Paul's Damascus road encounter with the risen Lord Christ. One could speculate that Luke has made use of these two separate, yet related, encounters as paradigmatic of the conversional experience as endemic to communion with those who were said to be people of "the Way" (see Acts 9:2); that is to say, transformation is a process that, while it has some point of initiation, is ongoing and must be nurtured in a community *of* and *on* "the Way." It is also of further intrigue that in both narratives (i.e., Emmaus and Damascus), the "eyes" must be "opened" (in the former case, the two disciples; in the latter case, Saul of Tarsus—the Apostle Paul) to the true identity of Jesus Messiah before confession can be made of the *truth* of both his person and his message.

In my use of these insights from the writing of Emile Mersch it is obvious that I share his contention; what may not be as obvious is how his observations have influenced my intended use of material from the Gospel of Luke (with the ever-present "sequel" in the background!). If, as I propose, there is a direct relationship between the category of *anamnesis* and the open-telling of the narrative of redemption, as essential to the overall sacramental integrity of the service of *Word* and *Sacrament*, then

---

31. Ibid., 73.

there must also be a sense in which the continuity of God's narrative of redemption—beyond the singularity of any one "book" of the Bible—can be affirmed in a canonical context. In other words, one need not read each and every portion of the Scripture in order to evoke an *anamnesis* of the Presence behind the grand narrative of redemption; this, it seems to me, is singularly evident in the liturgical pattern of the Church's Easter Vigil.

Even more to the point of my proposal, I find Luke's brilliant use of Gospel and "sequel" to be, in its own fashion, paradigmatic of the way in which the open-telling of any one part or "chapter" of the story of redemption cannot be restricted (or, I should say, by divine providence *has not been restricted*) to *one* particular literary form! Each and every piece of literature throughout the whole of the Church's canon bears the intensive (some would say divinely inspired) capacity to evoke *anamnesis* of the Presence behind redemption and the promise of future and complete restoration in the kingdom of God, and with particular force through an open-telling of that same "story" in the eucharistic-evangel. And Mersch's contention that "the distinctive note in St. Luke's account of the Mystical Body is its emphasis on the catholicity . . . of that Body" supports my contention that the narrative of redemption has universal implications as does the eucharistic-evangel.

A liturgy of *Word* and *Sacrament* in which both form and content are influenced by this more comprehensive perspective on the anamnetic character of the eucharistic-evangel would seek to incorporate in hymnody, sacred music, readings, proclamation, and practice the full panorama of redemptive history. As the highest form of liturgical thanksgiving, the eucharistic-evangel would express joyous praise to God (for creation), evoke and inspire remembrance (of redemption), and excite genuine expectation (of the coming kingdom of God) as components of that same *anamnesis*. The climactic fulfillment must always be the Christ-story, from which the believer will receive (as a gift of grace) the strengthening and enrichment of his or her identity in relation to the crucified, risen, reigning, and returning Lord Christ. The union of *spoken Word* and *visible Word* serves to disclose the *real presence* and true identity of Jesus Messiah—to, for, and with his followers in worship; this encounter with Christ transforms the personal and temporal identities of individual and community alike.

Moreover, while the union of *spoken Word* and *visible Word* in the eucharistic-evangel serves as a catalyst for transformation of identity, it also and at the same time deepens appreciation for what is the Church's (and each individual believer's) proper mission; personal and temporal identity narratives are not extrinsic to the full panorama of God's own redemptive history—rather, they are intrinsically and intricately interwoven into the very fabric of God's story which is still in process of being told. It may be that only as the story concludes will we come to a full appreciation of just how Christ has always been central to both our identity and mission as unfolding narratives, just as he has always stood at the center of God's own narrative of redemption. And so: "Every obedient administration of the anamnesis of Christ in the Holy Communion materializes the glory of the Triune God here on earth and on us . . . the glory of the Father, who sent the Son into our flesh for our reconciliation, the glory of the Incarnate One, whose sacrificial death is His glorification, the glory of the Eternal Spirit, who, as agape, enlivens the sacrifice of the Son in His *ekklesia*-body and preserves it to live to all eternity."[32]

We close this chapter with two admonitions, which encapsulate and express my concern as well; the first is from the Roman Catholic scholar Edward Schillebeeckx, and the second is from the Protestant scholar George Stroup. Schillebeeckx writes: "The essence of a sacrament lies in the outward shape of the rite as this participates in the sacramental spiritual meaning. . . . In other words the essence of a sacrament consists in the spiritual signification as this is made manifest in the liturgical shape of the rite."[33] And George Stroup writes: "Apart from the recital of Christian narrative the sacraments are vulnerable to distortion and misinterpretation, which is simply to say that the sacraments have their proper setting in the church's narratives of thanksgiving and confession."[34]

> And beginning with Moses and all the prophets, he interpreted to them in all the scriptures the things concerning himself. . . . When he was at table with them, he took the bread and blessed, and broke it, and gave it to them. And their eyes were opened and they recognized him. . . . And they rose that same hour and returned to Jerusalem. . . ." (Luke 24:27, 30–31, 33; RSV)

32. Brunner, *Worship in the Name of Jesus*, 196.
33. Schillebeeckx, *Christ, the Sacrament of the Encounter with God*, 96.
34. Stoup, *Promise of Narrative Theology*, 258.

FIVE

Transformation and Maintenance of a Distinctive Christian Identity

On the one hand, identity is essentially a name given when one is addressed: it is a calling, and often a promise. It becomes effectual when what lies in the name is brought into play. This is true both for individuals and for groups: John means "the Lord is gracious"; Jesus means "the Lord saves"; Israel means "the one who fought with God," which is said of Jacob and of the people (Gen. 32:28); church means "that which is addressed and called"; Christians are those who appeal to the authority of Christ (Acts 11:26).... Moreover, identity is also defined by recognition of the call of God. Individuals or groups acknowledge their identity by confessing God. Confession is correlative to calling (Pss. 95:7; 100:3; Rom. 10:9–13).... Confession of faith is at the same time an invitation for everyone to acknowledge God and live out the identity of believers. This invitation goes out to the ends of the earth (Pss. 96:1–3; 148; Acts 1:8).[1]

I HAVE ARGUED THROUGHOUT this essay that the liturgy of *Word* and *Sacrament* is essential to the transformation and maintenance of Christian identity. Such identity is determined *sine qua non* by the true identity of Jesus Messiah; therefore the genuine transformation and maintenance of Christian identity presupposes a proper identification of Jesus as the promised Messiah. As a corresponding point I have proposed that the liturgy of *Word* and *Sacrament* discloses the true identity (and therefore, "real

1. Clifford, *For the Communion of the Churches*, 202–3.

76

presence") of Jesus Messiah in a manner unparalleled by other liturgical events—with the possible exception of the Easter Vigil, which is celebrated on Holy Saturday in many traditions. It is not merely the sacred elements of bread and cup which disclose the true identity and "real presence" of Jesus Messiah; rather, the union of *spoken Word* and *visible Word* makes for a full disclosure of the Christ as the crucified, risen, reigning, and returning one who "fulfills the scriptures." As a consequence the union of *Word* and *Sacrament* is deemed essential to the transformative process and the spiritual welfare of Christian worship itself!

The necessary union of *spoken Word* and *visible Word* prevents the tendency to perceive the Eucharist itself (i.e., the breaking of bread and pouring of the cup) as an isolated, limited, and localized encounter with the *real presence* of Jesus Messiah; both scriptural interpretation and proclamation (*spoken Word*) and sacramental substance and ritual pattern (*visible Word*) are fundamental to the messianic identity of Jesus as the one who fulfills the whole of Scripture. To understand the Eucharist in any limited sense (e.g., concentration given to the bread and cup, the words of institution, or the *epiclesis*) will eventuate in the tendency to perceive the *anamnesis* and *real presence* itself as these isolated liturgical components alone; in this manner the *anamnesis* is too narrowly restricted to a liturgical focal point, and the theological reality of "real presence" confined to the boundaries of the eucharistic practice as narrowly defined. I believe that such practice and comprehension has only diminished the profound nature of the eucharistic-evangel, creating as well the possibility of viewing the sacramental action(s) as "magical" rather than as "mystery."

If, as I have argued throughout this essay, the eucharistic-evangel—as the liturgy of *Word* and *Sacrament*—discloses the true identity of Jesus Messiah, then it becomes evident that the entire worship event must remain open to the possibility of his self-disclosure in the power of the Holy Spirit. And this affirmation raises some important questions: Is the identity of Christ restricted to the elements of bread and cup? There can be little doubt that passion and death (liturgically re-presented) stand at the heart of the identity of Christ, but are they the *only* mediums of his identification? Were not his life, teachings, and ministry of grace equally revelatory of his true identity as the one who fulfilled the Scriptures? Are we not compelled, therefore, to assert a more panoramic identification of Jesus Messiah, which presupposes a more holistic knowledge of redemptive history, beginning with Adam and moving toward consummation in the coming reign of God? My position is to affirm the more holistic ap-proach to the christological realities of this sacramental drama, as well as the consequent transformation and maintenance of identity. The depth of Christian identity (both individual and communal) cannot be limited to any one particular aspect or characteristic of Christ as he is *re*-presented to us in the gospel accounts and in the epistolary of the New Testament (not to mention the book of Revelation!). Christian identity is informed and shaped by the whole of Christ, made present to the believer and wor-shipping body in the power of the Holy Spirit by *Word* and *Sacrament*—by *spoken* and *visible Word*.[2]

The holistic pattern of redemptive history and the flow of salvation history, as embodied in the witness of the Old and New Testaments, serve as integral to a comprehensive and proper identification of Jesus Messiah. The liturgy of *Word* and *Sacrament* discloses his comprehensive identity through both the open-telling of redemptive history (*spoken Word*) and the sacramental act *(visible Word)*. The eucharistic-evangel will be experienced in all its profundity and power as a disclosure event to the extent that the en-tire worship includes the necessary union of *spoken* and *visible Word*. What this affirmation intends is quite radical; so much is that the case, some may think it nothing more than hyperbole. Nevertheless, I would contend that the worshipper cannot comprehend the "new creation" in Christ (integral to his identity) without first having an appreciation of the "first creation" as recorded in Genesis; or adequately comprehend the beauty of the prom-ise given in Christ without a prior appreciation of the promise made to Abraham; or comprehend the significance of the "Second Adam" without appreciable knowledge of the "First Adam"; or fully grasp the importance of the "new covenant" without prior appreciation of the "old covenant." The proper identification of the *real presence* can only be enhanced by such an

2. In conclusion to his own discussion of the differences in eucharistic theology be-tween the reformers Luther, Zwingli, and Calvin (et al.), Otto Weber writes: ". . . Calvin . . . does not see the work of the Spirit restricted to making us certain of what 'in and of itself' is already given. He does not refer us to the 'remembrance' which takes place with us, as does Zwingli. . . . He points out that Christ himself is present in us in the Spirit, that through the Spirit we are lifted up to him—through God's Spirit and not through our spiritual ability. The presence of Christ in the Lord's Supper and elsewhere is a spiritual presence, and for that very reason it is a real presence. . . . The Son of God is completely with us. But he is simultaneously outside of the humanity which he has assumed. He becomes a servant. But he remains the Lord. He becomes spatial and temporal, but he remains supreme over space and time. Calvin thus returns to paradox." Weber, *Founda-tions of Dogmatics*, 2:132.

open-telling of redemptive history through proclamation (*spoken Word*) in union with the sacramental act (*visible Word*).

Within the framework of such a liturgical structure, *anamnesis* is no longer restricted to any one particular event of redemptive history (e.g., "Calvary") but embodies the entire ebb and flow of God's salvific activity on behalf of creature and creation. Furthermore, *anamnesis* is not limited merely to the recollections of historical events; rather it becomes the setting for the *reactualization* of the *real presence* of the one who was, is, and will always be the personal force behind such redemptive events. The implication of this position for the *anamnesis* of the Christ-event (as the double kenosis of incarnation and obedient suffering, the ministry of forgiveness and reconciliation, table fellowship with sinners, the death, resurrection, ascension, and sending of the *Paraclete*), is the recognition of the true identity of Jesus Messiah as the climactic fulfillment of the scriptural witness to God's plan of salvation (i.e., as disclosed in the writings of the Law, Prophets, and the Writings).

The full (true) identity of Jesus Messiah is perceived as the one who embodies and brings to actualization the fullness of redemptive history from creation to consummated kingdom, from origin to aim (*telos*), from Alpha to Omega. The comprehensive (true) identity of Jesus Messiah includes his incarnation, life, suffering, death, resurrection, ascension, and reign at the right hand of the Father; it is *this* characteristic of Jesus' identity as Messiah which is distinctively his own. This truth of Christ Jesus directs or impacts in immediate fashion my proposal that the liturgy of *Word* and *Sacrament*—as the union of *spoken* and *visible Word*—provides the worshipful setting for the revelation of the "real presence" and true identity of Jesus as the Christ of God. Furthermore, because this union forms the distinctive dimension of the identity of the Christ, it also serves as the creative force in the formation of a distinctive form of Christian worship event, in which fellowship in and with this Christ is both desired and actualized. And this liturgical and sacramental encounter with the "real presence" and true identity of the Messiah—and in the power of the Holy Spirit—transforms and serves to maintain the distinctive identity and mission of the believer in symmetry with that of Christ himself. Yet, what is it that marks the Christian as having a distinctive identity? Perhaps a more helpful phrasing of the same question is: What are the "marks" of a distinctive Christian identity?[3]

3. Most readers are, I would assume, familiar with the so-called marks of the Church as "one, holy, catholic, and apostolic." In a similar sense I am advocating that

A comprehensive characterization of Christian identity would include those sacerdotal events that mark the individual believer within the community in a significant way; while baptism and confirmation represent those sacred rites in which the individual's identity is marked in a specific fashion, they are also and at the same time events which are celebrated but once in the life of any believer.[4] The eucharistic-evangel, on the other hand, represents that sacred and worshipful event that establishes and sustains the distinctiveness of Christian identity beyond the immediacy of baptism and confirmation; this is the sacrament of successive transformation in which the believer's identity is being conformed to the "image of Christ" and through which his or her relationship to the "body of Christ" is deepened in an irreversible bond of love. I recognize that for most Protestant traditions confirmation is *not* considered a sacrament (whereas baptism and the Eucharist *are* sacraments for the greatest number of Protestant confessions); nevertheless, there is a sense in which, even where confirmation is not thought to be *a* sacrament, it is treated as sacramental in character (i.e., in the bestowal of the Holy Spirit, and in the confirmation of faith in Christ as a gift of grace). It is not wild speculation to suggest that baptism,[5] confirmation, and Eucharist—as "means of grace"—be comprehended as evidence of the transformative, healing, redeeming, reconciling, and forgiving presence of God (in Christ) and in the power of the Holy Spirit. To

the distinctive identity of the Christian believer is associated with particular marks, and these characteristic marks are as essential to one's Christian identity as the four marks of the Church have been in distinguishing her from all other forms of institutional life or historic organization. The proposed marks of Christian identity are also, like those of the Church, intended to be broad enough to allow for the presence of other characteristics one may associate with Christian identity, just as each of the four marks of the Church serves as a generalization under which one could delineate any number of related characteristics (e.g., "catholic" as intended to convey both *universal* and historically *holistic* characteristics).

4. I am fully aware that this position runs counter to my Anabaptist brethren; nevertheless, I would still contend that "re-baptism" adds nothing significant to the identity of the Christian that has not already been graciously provided in his or her "first" baptism.

5. In addressing the sacramental characteristics of baptism, T. F. Torrance writes: "Baptism is into the name of the whole Christ; not just into the name of the dying and rising Christ, but the Christ who was born of the Virgin Mary, who was baptized at the Jordan, in fact the whole historical Jesus. Baptism into Christ includes therefore a sharing in His birth and His human life, as well as in His death and resurrection." Torrance, *Conflict and Agreement in the Church*, 2:128. This observation bears directly on my proposal in that it focuses attention, more than most, in this particular sacrament on a more holistic presentation of life transformed in relation to the fullness of Christ's identity and not any one aspect of Christ's character alone.

speak of "grace" (in this manner) is, therefore, to speak of the *real presence* in the broadest sense of that theological categorization of sacramental disclosure.

Baptism

Jesus was baptized by John in the waters of the Jordan River, marking a vital transition from the historical and theological period of "old covenant" to that of the "new covenant," from the age of the Law, the Prophets, and the Writings to that of Christ as the fulfillment of the same in their entirety.[6] It is no accident of fate that this particular baptism was administered in what we might call a "public" setting—even though out in the wilderness regions surrounding the holy city of Jerusalem. That is vitally important, or so it seems to me, for the way in which the church came to understand the rite of baptism as more than some private rite of passage; this event was, even though restricted to the environs of the community of faith, an event intended to serve as a witness to the wider world (i.e., the "public" realm) of the continuing unfolding of God's great plan of salvation being manifest in one life at a time, yet with much broader significance.[7]

For the Christian believer, baptism marks the true transition from the "old" life in captivity to sin and its consequence(s) to the "new" life in grace (yet as *simul jutus et peccator*). In the words of the Apostle Paul, "when we were baptized we went into the tomb with [Christ] and joined him in death

6. "Jesus himself and probably some of his disciples had submitted to John's baptism. When Jesus' resurrection and the Pentecostal experience of the Spirit launched the mission of the gospel, those granted faith by the apostolic proclamation became penitents exactly in John's sense, though that was not all they became. The apostles welcomed these penitents with the same rite by which they (or some of them) had themselves repented. Thereby baptism became what it had not been for John: an initiation." Braaten and Jenson, *Christian Dogmatics*, 2:316.

7. "... it is only through and within the Church created by the corporate Baptism of the Spirit at Pentecost, and drawn and established within the fulfillment of the Covenant-will of God in the obedient life and death of Christ, that when from generation to generation the Church in obedience to Christ's command baptizes in water, others are added to the Church that they may share in what has already taken place for them and live in the power of the Name of Christ, as members of the Body of Christ who was crucified for them and raised again in justification for them. Thus the Baptism of the individual, child or adult, is not a new Baptism, but an initiation into and a sharing in the One Baptism common to Christ and His Church, wrought out in Christ alone but bestowed upon the Church as it is yoked together with Him through the Baptism of the Spirit." Torrance, *Conflict and Agreement in the Church*, 2:115.

[to sin], so that as Christ was raised from the dead by the Father's glory, we too might live a new life" (Rom 6:4b; Jerusalem Bible); furthermore, in baptism the Christian is "taken out of the power of darkness" and given a place "in the kingdom of the Son" (Col 1:13; Jerusalem Bible).[8] Through the sacrament of baptism Christian identity is marked, once and for all time, by the fundamental and distinct identity of Jesus Messiah; baptism is the concise moment of the initial transformative event in the life of the one baptized, and may go unnoticed on a self-conscious level (obviously the case in infant baptism, but I would contend the same could be said of those who have been baptized in adulthood at any stage of life if this sacramental event is perceived as little more than a "rite of passage"). "Baptism is the sign of new life through Jesus Christ. It unites the one baptized with Christ and his people."[9] We would not want to underestimate the essential aspect of the *corporate* dimension to this identity; when I spoke earlier of the "public" nature of this sacrament, "public" was intended to convey the meaning of both the church (as a "public" setting in its corporate nature) and the wider "world" (the domain of ministry and mission in a "public" setting beyond the boundaries of the local congregation).[10]

---

8. As evidenced in the footnote above, T. F. Torrance takes a more holistic approach to the sacrament of baptism than is normally argued and extends this "new life" to an incorporation into the whole of the life of Christ and not merely to that of his death and resurrection exclusively. He writes: ". . . there are not two acts of regeneration, incorporation, etc. but only one, that which has already been wrought out in Jesus Christ and in which we are given to share through the Spirit, so that it is in Christ that we are born again through sharing in His birth, and it is in Him that we are converted through sharing in His obedient life, and in Him that we are resurrected through sharing in His resurrection. He was not born on earth for His own sake, but for our sake. His birth for our sake was part of His reconciling and redeeming work, and Baptism is grounded primarily upon that basic event, His incorporation into our humanity, and therefore upon His obedience unto the death of the Cross in expiation of our sin and guilt, and in His resurrection out of our mortality as the New Man." Ibid., 2:118.

9. World Council of Churches, *Baptism, Eucharist, and Ministry*, 2.

10. "The remarkable gifts said by the New Testament to be given at baptism are simply the privileges claimed by a remarkable community. In that the church is the community of the 'justified' and 'sanctified,' baptism justifies and sanctifies (1 Cor. 1:26–31; 6:8–11). In that the church fulfills the prophecies of a kingdom of priests or a nation of prophets, baptism appears as the requisite anointing (Heb. 10:22; 1 John 2:18–27). In that the church is persecuted and raised above the persecutors, baptism 'saves' (1 Peter 1:3–21). In that the church is the bride of Christ, baptism is the bride's toilette (Eph. 5:25–27)." Braaten and Jenson, *Christian Dogmatics*, 2:319.

Like the eucharistic-evangel, this sacred event that "marks" a distinctive Christian identity contains an ethical dimension as an expression of the transformation in process throughout the life of the believer, so that:

> As they grow in the Christian life of faith, baptized believers demonstrate that humanity can be regenerated and liberated. They have a common responsibility, here and now, to bear witness together to the Gospel of Christ, the liberator of all human beings. The context of this common witness is the Church and the world. Within a fellowship of witness and service, Christians discover the full significance of one baptism as the gift of God to all God's people. Likewise, they acknowledge that baptism has ethical implications which not only call for personal sanctification, but also motivate the Christians to strive for the realization of the will of God in *all realms of life* (Rom. 6:9ff.; Gal. 3:27-28; 1 Peter 2:21–4:6).[11]

Thus baptism is shown to have implications on both individual and corporate levels of life and the identity of the individual believer is essentially joined to that of the community.

Confirmation

The Gospel according to St. Mark records the events following the baptism of Jesus by John in the river Jordan: "As soon as He came up out of the water, He saw the heavens being torn open and the Spirit descending to Him like a dove. And a voice came from heaven: You are My beloved Son; I take delight in You!" (Mark 1:10–11).

The "descending" of the Spirit following Jesus' baptism marks the moment of commission to service and ministry in the public setting. However, this is not to say that Jesus had no prior knowledge of his mission and purpose; rather, the Spirit descends to *confirm* his identity, ministry, and mission. The presence of the Spirit "marks" the identity of Jesus as that which is then disclosed in the words of "a voice [that] came from heaven" as "beloved Son" and "delight" of God; Christ enters the world in service to the Father in the powerful presence of the Spirit.

Confirmation impresses the formation of Christian identity in a parallel fashion. In the service of confirmation (as the confirmation of baptism, faith, and ministry), the individual believer, empowered by the Holy Spirit, enters self-consciously into the full mission and ministry of God's

11. World Council of Churches, *Baptism, Eucharist, and Ministry*, 4.

Church in the world (the "public setting") and as a self-acknowledged "child of God" committed to Christ. As the Spirit of the Father and Son "descends," the identity of the disciple of the Christ of the Gospel is confirmed; this confirmation is a communal event and the incentive to remain open (within the community of faith) to the further transformation of identity as the one confirmed is "conformed" to the image of Christ in the "image" (read: *identity*) of Jesus Messiah and spiritually empowered (by *charisma*) for participation in the mission and ministry of Christ in and through the "body" of believers. Where this event is too often associated with individual choice, I stress the communal nature of the event as the venue of accountability for proper—or faithful!—employment of the "gifts of the Spirit" for the furtherance of the Gospel and to the glory of God. To place confirmation within the overall plan of identity transformation may ameliorate the tendency among many to view this event as the vehicle for participation in the Eucharist; there is a sense in which baptism, confirmation, and eucharistic-evangel must be bound together in order to avoid the perception that they are merely "steps" in the progress of developing Christian identity. I am merely asserting their unity in the process of transformation and maintenance of Christian identity; their interrelatedness is essential as each contributes in a substantial way to the overall process of transformation. What differentiates them is not so much the contribution made to the process, although such contributions are somewhat unique; it is, rather, the fact that whereas baptism and confirmation, as liturgical events, are celebrated but once in the life of the believer, the eucharistic-evangel is to be celebrated with far greater frequency (I argue for weekly celebration!). I will return to this theme in my closing remarks.

So, there is a sense in which confirmation, like baptism, is a singular event in the transformative process and the maintenance of identity as well. As stated above, as liturgical events, confirmation and baptism are celebrated once; but the significant distinction between the two is that confirmation of faith and practice (i.e., mission and ministry) must occur repeatedly in and throughout the Christian life. As affirmed in *Baptism, Eucharist, and Ministry*:

> [Confirmation] is related not only to momentary experience, but to life-long growth into Christ. Those baptized [and confirmed] are called upon to reflect the glory of the Lord as they are *transformed* by the power of the Holy Spirit (2 Cor. 3:18). The life of the Christian is necessarily one of continuing struggle [see Mark 1:13a!] yet

also of continuing experience of grace [see Mark 1:13b!]. In this new relationship, the baptized [and confirmed] live for the sake of Christ, of his Church and of the world which he loves, while they wait in hope for the manifestation of God's new creation and for the time when God will be all in all (Rom. 8:18–24; 1 Cor. 15:22–28, 49–57).[12]

Attention is drawn to the eschatological dimension in the above quote (i.e., "while they wait in hope"), which is also evident in the eucharistic-evangel! This eschatological dimension is fundamental to the distinctive (true) identity of Jesus Messiah (as the one who has come and will "return"—the affirmation of both first and second advents as essential to Christ's identity). The eschatological dimension is, therefore, an essential "mark" of what is a distinctive characteristic of the identity of the Christian disciple transformed in the "image" of Christ. Furthermore, the "already" and "not yet" dimension of identity parallels the theological affirmation of the Christian as *simul jutus et peccator*! There is a perfection of identity attributable to Christ and Christ alone; a similar perfection awaits the Christian as an eschatological reality (which could be said of the Church as well!), remembering that while this is held in "hope," as the Apostle Paul once wrote, "hope will not disappoint us" (Rom 5:5) as our reality at present is "Christ in you, the hope of glory" (Col 2:27).

Personal and corporate prayer, the public and private reading of Scripture, personal and corporate devotion and worship, are practices of faith through which the empowering Spirit also transforms the identity of the disciple and community at large. In this manner as well the identity of the individual believer is transformed in the "image" of Jesus Messiah: "Participation in Christ's death and resurrection is inseparably linked with the receiving of the Spirit . . . the gift of the Spirit is to be found in the anointing with chrism and/or the imposition of hands and a declaration that the persons baptized have acquired a *new identity* as sons and daughters of God, and as members of the Church, called to be witnesses to the Gospel."[13]

Eucharistic-Evangel

What I have proposed throughout this essay will now be stated in a summary form, which will undoubtedly entail some redundancy; it is my

12. Ibid.

13. Ibid., 6.

contention, however, that this summation is essential and conclusive to this chapter in which the subject has been the transformation and maintenance of a distinctive Christian identity as related to the three fundamental liturgical events (i.e., baptism, confirmation, and the eucharistic-evangel) in the process of identity formation.

As I have stated throughout this essay, the eucharistic-evangel is that liturgical event which represents the most profound medium in the transformation and maintenance of a distinctive Christian identity, constituting the third and final "mark," primarily because it is *here* in this liturgical event that *anamnesis* and *real presence* converge in the transformative process. It is in the context of this liturgical event that the worshipper (and gathered community)—through the liturgy of *Word* and *Sacrament*—encounter and are encountered by the fullness of the identity of Jesus Messiah (his true identity) as *real presence*. Furthermore, this sacramental event reaffirms the identity transformation begun at baptism and strengthened in confirmation: "Baptism [and confirmation of faith and practice] needs to be constantly reaffirmed. The most obvious form for such reaffirmation is the celebration of the eucharist."[14]

There are various levels of *anamnesis* operative in the liturgy of *Word* and *Sacrament*, but two are of central importance: (1) *anamnesis* as actualization of one's personal and temporal identity; and (2) *anamnesis* as actualization of the personal, temporal, and eternal identity of Jesus Messiah. The identity of the Christian, when encountering the true identity of Jesus Messiah (as *real presence* in *spoken* and *visible* Word), is transformed: "The deepest reality is the total being of Christ who comes to us in order to feed us and *transform* our entire being!"[15] In my exposition of the Lucan narrative I discussed in detail the significance of maintaining the union of *Word* and *Sacrament* as that distinctively Christian liturgical event that discloses the full and distinct (true) identity of Jesus Messiah (i.e., as the crucified, risen, reigning, returning one who fulfills the whole of Scripture). Therefore, it is this liturgical event that marks the distinctive nature of Christian identity as well:

> Since the *anamnesis* of Christ is the very content of the preached Word as it is of the eucharistic meal, each reinforces the other. The celebration of the Eucharist properly includes the proclamation of the Word. . . . United (in this way) to our Lord and in communion

14. Ibid., 5.

15. World Council of Churches, *Baptism, Eucharist, Ministry*, 12.

> with all the saints and martyrs, we are renewed in the covenant sealed by the blood of Christ. . . . In the eucharist, Christ empowers us to live with him, to suffer with him and to pray through him as justified sinners, joyfully and freely fulfilling his will.[16]

In the liturgy of *Word* and *Sacrament*, the climactic fulfillment of the eucharistic-evangel is the point at which the bread is broken and the cup poured out and elevated ("And their eyes were opened and they recognized him," Luke 24:31a). Here the worshipper and community gathered at altar table experience the precise *anamnesis* of Christ Jesus as the one who was broken for human transgressions, poured out for the forgiveness of sins, and elevated to the right hand of God. In this way "the presence of Christ is clearly the center of the eucharist."[17] This one, whose true identity is disclosed as *real presence*, is the one broken open so as to make himself available to/for the worshipper (and community/in community), pouring out his identity and thus sharing it—as grace—with both individual and community. In the present, temporal, and personal realities of the worshipper (and community), Christ shares his Spirit (as gift of both Father and Son)—the Spirit of servanthood and obedience to the Father, the Spirit who empowers mission and ministry, the Spirit who sustains faith and enables hope to abide throughout the tumult of life:

> Solidarity in the Eucharistic communion of the body of Christ and responsible care of Christians for one another and the world find specific expression in the liturgies: in the mutual forgiveness of sins; in the sign of peace; intercession for all; the eating and drinking together; the taking of the elements to the sick and those in prison or the celebration of the eucharist with them. All these manifestations of love in the eucharist are directly related to Christ's own testimony as a servant, in whose servanthood Christians themselves participate. As God in Christ has entered into the human situation, so eucharistic liturgy is near to the concrete and particular situations of men and women. . . . The place of such ministry between the table and the needy properly testifies to the redeeming presence of Christ in the world.[18]

Recall those striking words of the Apostle Paul: "Now those who belong to Christ have crucified the flesh with its passions and desires" and now

16. Ibid.
17. Ibid., 13.
18. Ibid., 14.

"since we live by the Spirit, we must also follow the Spirit" (Gal 5:24–25). The distinctive identity of the Christian (i.e., as one who has crucified the flesh and is living by the Spirit) conforms to the distinctive (true) identity of Jesus Messiah (i.e., as the crucified and risen one). It is *anamnesis* as *real presence* which will evoke more than mere identification with the events of Christ's life; rather, the identity of the individual and community are transformed through such encounter, and conform to the "image" of Christ disclosed as uniquely his own, his distinctive identity disclosed in *Word* and *Sacrament*.

The twofold dimension to *anamnesis* (as stated above) establishes the following pattern: (1) who I *was* (lost in sin and captive to the sting of death), who Jesus *was* (the Mediator, Reconciler, and Redeemer, bringing salvation and the promise of resurrection and eternal life in the coming kingdom of God); (2) who I *am* (as *simul justus et peccator*), who Jesus Christ *is* (the Lord and Sanctifier of my life); and (3) who I *will be* (a guest at the royal feast in the kingdom of God), who Jesus Christ *will be* (the slain and victorious Lamb of God who presides at the wedding feast in the kingdom of God—see Rev 19:5–10). There is genuine correspondence between the past, present, and future dynamics and realities of Christ and of those who belong to Christ, but here I am speaking only in terms of identity; this is not so much an *ontological* (i.e., state of being) affirmation, as such would be well beyond what could be considered responsible as an assertion; it is an affirmation of the way in which the transformative process unfolds in a correspondence to the entire event of incarnation, passion, resurrection, and return of Christ as endemic to his true identity and made present in the *anamnesis* of the eucharistic-evangel.[19]

The desire to broaden the basis upon which the category of *anamnesis* is to be interpreted has significant implications for the category of *real presence* as well. The dual character of *anamnesis* being advocated in this essay advances the concept of *real presence* as a genuinely transformative encounter (both "in" and "with" Christ): "In the eucharistic meal, in eating and drinking of the bread and wine, Christ grants communion with

19. "The Church at the Eucharist is a structured community, a community listening to the word of God, a community in continuity with the preaching, ministry, death, and resurrection of its Lord, a community looking forward to the coming of the Kingdom, a community conscious of its sinfulness and repentant of its sins, a community convinced of the power of God's grace, a community ready to serve others, i.e., to carry out 'the breaking of bread' beyond the Church, and a community here and now open to the presence of the Lord and Spirit." McBrien, *Catholicism*, 2:767.

himself. God himself acts, giving life to the body of Christ and renewing each member."[20] Note the reference to both individual and corporate dimensions of this sacramental encounter; it is this characteristic which gives the eucharistic-evangel its distinctive dimension (one that sets it apart from both baptism and confirmation as "marks" of a distinctive Christian identity). For while it is necessary for baptism and confirmation to take place within the worshipping body as testimony to their corporate nature, "it is in the eucharist that the community of God's people is fully manifested."[21]

The gathered assembly (as the "body of Christ") shares in the *anamnetic* experience of transformation; as the liturgy of *Word* and *Sacrament* unfolds, with the climactic fulfillment disclosed in the *precise* moment of bread broken and cup poured out and elevated, which are then distributed and shared, the oneness of the bread and cup (body and blood) in communion actualizes the unity of the "body of Christ," under the Lordship of him who remains her "Head." Under the *anamnetic* experience, the assembly recognizes, acknowledges, and confesses the *real presence* of the one who embraces and transforms their lives. On the temporal level, his past, present, and future permeates their own, and in the power of the Holy Spirit imbues their own time with meaning and *missional* purpose:

> As it is entirely the gift of God, the eucharist brings into the present age a new reality which transforms Christians into the image of Christ and therefore makes them his effective witnesses. . . . The eucharistic community is nourished and strengthened for confessing by word and action the Lord Jesus Christ who gave his life for the salvation of the world. As it becomes one people, sharing the meal of the one Lord, the eucharistic assembly must be concerned for gathering also those who are at present beyond its visible limits, because Christ invited to his feast all for whom he died. Insofar as Christians cannot invite in full fellowship around the same table to eat the same food and drink the same cup, their missionary witness is weakened at both the individual and corporate levels.[22]

The eucharistic-evangel is thus to be perceived as much more than *anamnesis* of "the night on which he was betrayed," and the events of the fateful evening and week of Passion. It is rather *anamnesis* (1) of the entire panorama of God's redemptive history from creation to eschaton as such,

20. World Council of Churches, *Baptism, Eucharist, and Ministry*, 10.

21. Ibid., 14.

22. Ibid., 15.

and is therefore "the Church's effective proclamation of God's mighty acts and promises,"[23] and (2) of that central Christ-event "with all that he has accomplished for us and for all creation (in his incarnation, servanthood, ministry, teaching, suffering, sacrifice, resurrection, ascension, and sending forth of the Holy Spirit)."[24] In this sense "the Church, gratefully recalling God's mighty acts of redemption, beseeches God to give the benefits of these acts to every human being. . . . It is the memorial of all that God has done for the salvation of the world."[25] The implications of such an interpretation are far-reaching for liturgical theology in an ecumenical setting. The *ordinary* time of human existence is transformed with a *sacral* temporality; the temporal and personal dimensions of one's identity (including such things as work, play, study, leisure) are taken up into the panorama of God's redemptive temporality. The events of one's life (past, present, and future), which give form, content, and meaning to identity, are taken up into the universal scope of God's continuing actions in and for the world.

It is not that I merely "remember" what it must have been like for Abraham, Isaac, and Jacob, for Joseph or Moses and the children of Israel, or for the disciples of Jesus. It is not that, as a community of faith, we somehow (through some Herculean regression) "remember" what it was like for the children of Israel in captivity and exodus, in exile and return, or for the Church in its nascent form. Rather, the one who was present to and for these individuals and communities of faith is actually disclosed as the very same *real presence* with and for me and the corporate body in which I fellowship, of which I am a member. The same creative and redemptive actions, and the *real presence* of the one associated with those actions, are together *anamnetically* revealed. Incorporation "in Christ" is one way to speak of membership in the Church (language often associated with baptism); identification "with Christ" is yet another way to speak of the relationship between individual/community and Christ (language often associated with confirmation); what I am referring to throughout this essay is a radical internalization "of Christ," which demands openness as receptivity on the part of both individual and community. This transformational encounter is a gift of grace and under the directive of the Holy Spirit, it is a

23. Ibid., 11.
24. Ibid.
25. Ibid.

mystery that is to be upheld and revered, even though it can never be fully comprehended at its deepest dimension.[26]

The following is a quote from John W. Nevin's *Mystical Presence*, and is being offered at this point to demonstrate the *organic* nature of the transformative process being discussed in this essay; I want to make clear that this reality of being "in" Christ, "with" Christ, and having Christ "in" the believer is far more than some instrumental approach to the union proposed. In his discussion of the Eucharist, Nevin asserts that one of the more powerful images Christ employs to speak of the organic nature of the relationship between himself and the believer is that of the "vine" and the "branches." Nevin writes:

> The union between the vine and the branches is organic. They are not placed together in an outward and merely mechanical way. The vine reveals itself in the branches; and the branches have no vitality apart from the vine. All form one and the same life. . . . Christ dwells in his people by the Holy Spirit, and is formed in them the hope of glory. They grow up into him in all things; and are transformed into the same image, from glory to glory, as by the Spirit of the Lord. The life of Christ is reproduced in them, under the same true human character that belongs to it in his own person.[27]

26. John Williamson Nevin writes this: "The *whole* glorified Christ subsists and acts *in the Spirit*. Under this form his nature communicates itself to his people. They, too, to the same extent, are made thus to live and walk *in the Spirit*, both in soul and body. Christ lives in them, and they live in Christ; and still, as their sanctification proceeds, this mutual indwelling becomes more intimate and complete, until, at last, in the resurrection, they appear fully transformed into the same image, 'as by the Spirit of the Lord' (2 Cor. 3:18; see, also, Philippians 3:21)." Nevin, *Mystical Presence*, 235.

27. Ibid., 236.

SIX

The Contribution
of John Williamson Nevin

The Mystical Presence

So the acts of the incarnate Word belong to his person as a whole. Not as though his humanity separately considered could be said to exercise the functions of his divinity; for this is a false distinction in this case; and we have just as little reason to say that the divinity thus separately considered ever exercises the same functions. They are exercised by the theanthropic person of the Mediator, as one and indivisible. If then Christ's life be conveyed over to the persons of his people at all, in a real and not simply figurative way, it *must* be so carried over under a human form, including both the constituents of humanity, body as well as soul; and the new bodily existence thus produced, must be con- sidered—independently of all local connection—a continuation in the strictest sense of Christ's life under the same form.[1]

W E CLOSED OUT THE last chapter with a quote from John Williamson Nevin, one of the premier theologians of the nineteenth-century movement in America that came to be known as the Mercersburg theology, which was instrumental in the founding of what later became Lancaster Theological Seminary and was one of the more ecumenical movements of its era. In this chapter I undertake an exposition of applicable sections

1. Nevin, *Mystical Presence*, 153.

of what is arguably Nevin's most famous work, *The Mystical Presence*, not so much as an endorsement of my proposal, but as a resource, from the Reformed tradition in North America, holding promise for making a trenchant *contribution* to my proposal from a profound piece of sacramental theology. I have come to appreciate the depth of the ecumenical concern evident in and throughout the writings of Nevin, Schaff, and others of the Mercersburg theology—and continue to follow, with great interest, the contemporary exponents of this same theological tradition. Few traditions in the North American setting can claim the highly sacramental characteristic evident throughout much of the theological reflection and liturgical writings provided by scholars, past and present, from this particular school of thought.

Throughout this chapter I am indebted to the critical work of Richard E. Wentz, which is titled *John Williamson Nevin: American Theologian*—arguably one of the best introductions to the thought of Nevin in the context of the church in North America, and in particular as a Reformed theologian with strong sacramental leanings and "ecumenical" interests. The primary source focus is on Nevin's *Mystical Presence*, which has been rightly claimed a theological classic in the North American setting of the Church catholic.

Published in 1846, and acknowledged to be one of Nevin's finest pieces of theological reflection, *The Mystical Presence* is also remarkable in its contribution of a mediating position in the eucharistic theology and ongoing debate of his time (and perhaps ours!), offering as it does an alternative to the prevailing options of either transubstantiation (primarily Roman Catholic) and consubstantiation (primarily Lutheran). Nevin's argument, however, is not so much with either of the two interpretations of *real presence* or the confessional bodies represented by the respective positions. His more pressing issue of concern is with the distortion of the more orthodox or *primitive Reformed* position, as a position evidenced in the teaching of John Calvin, select confessional documents, and grounded in the sacramental theology of the early Church catholic. Nevin is also critical of the tendency to polarize the subjective (*inward, spiritual*) and objective (*outward, corporeal*) dimensions of what I am calling the eucharistic-evangel— a polarization exemplified in the teachings of rationalism and those radical forms of pietism that often eventuate in sectarianism.

There is no way to determine whether or not Nevin thought his sacramental thesis in *The Mystical Presence* novel, but it is clear in both style and content that he intended to argue for the reclamation of a position on the eucharistic *real presence* that would be in harmony with the record of the New Testament, the writings of the early Church fathers, and select theologians from the Reformed tradition. In what is arguably typical of Mercersburg theology, Nevin harmonizes the theological concepts of incarnational, christological, sacramental, and ecclesiological foci. It is this characteristic of Nevin's writing that can be said to support the claim to its *catholicity*, demonstrating as well the promise and potential contributions of his theological reflections for contemporary ecumenical dialogue and debate. It is this same characteristic that also holds such great promise in providing a theological rationale and basis for my contention that the eucharistic-evangel be perceived as fundamental to the transformation and maintenance of a distinctive Christian identity, even across confessional and denominational boundary markers!

This brief chapter will achieve two modest goals: (1) having provided an overview of Nevin's entire work (i.e., *The Mystical Presence*), I will propose ways in which his project contributes to issues and concerns evident in the continuing dialogue and debate of the wider ecumenical movement; and (2) I will highlight the salient features of *The Mystical Presence*, suggesting their applicability to the narrower purpose of supporting my contention that advances can be made in ecumenical dialogue by focusing on issues beyond those that continue to thwart and stigmatize ecumenical conversations regarding the Eucharist; here I will return to my contention that advances can be made along the lines of those offered in my proposal. I will then close this chapter with one or two observations of a more general nature, evincing some of the ways in which Nevin's theological reflections in *The Mystical Presence* are of continuing value to the Church catholic, beyond what could be called their obvious historical merit.

In his intellectual biography of Nevin, Wentz states that *The Mystical Presence* represents Nevin's "struggle to comprehend the historical significance of the Incarnation of Jesus Christ."[2] Together with, and in some fashion directly related to, the larger issues of an incarnational theology, Wentz contends that the prevailing philosophical and theological concern for Nevin was the effort to clarify the relationship between the inward (*subjective, spiritual*) and the outward (*objective, corporeal*) dimensions of the sacrament, in particular, and Christian belief and practice, in general: "For John Nevin, a substantive altering of history had taken place in the Incarnation of Jesus Christ, the significance of which is advanced and

2. Wentz, *John Williamson Nevin*, 10.

constructively celebrated in the Eucharist. 'We have no right,' he said, 'to set the inward in opposition to the outward, the spiritual in opposition to the corporeal, in religion.'"—by which he meant Christianity as at once the "individual and general" of what religion itself means.[3] One of the more promising characteristics of Nevin's approach is to move the entire conversation regarding the doctrine of the *real presence* beyond the confining terminology of localization or the reductive language of commemoration, emotionality, or sacrificial reenactment. With Nevin "the sacramental doctrine of the primitive Reformed Church inseparably connected with the idea of an inward living union between believers and Christ, in virtue of which they are incorporated into his very nature, and made to subsist with him by the power of a common life."[4]

Wentz offers an insightful analysis of the phrase Nevin uses throughout *The Mystical Presence*, "separately considered," and states that "whether speaking of moral union, national life, elements of the Eucharist, or the life of Christ, Nevin uses the expression in order to emphasize the relational quality of all aspects of human existence."[5] In his desire to advance comprehension of and appreciation for the concept of *real presence* beyond localized language of either transubstantiation or consubstantiation, "Nevin reminds readers that the presence 'is not such as to identify the body of Christ in any way with sacramental symbols, *separately considered.*' It is not bound to the bread and wine, but to the act of eating and drinking."[6] Of course, for Nevin, this act of eating and drinking represent participation in the whole life of Christ, so that "the believer partakes of Christ, not only in figure, but in fact; not of his benefits simply, but of his actual life; not of his life as divine merely, but of his human life, as denoted by his body and blood."[7]

The debate between Lutheran and Reformed theologians on the issue of *real presence* revolves, at least in part, around the differences located in the teachings of Luther and Calvin, respectively. While Luther argued for the *ubiquity* of Christ's body, and of his presence *in, with, and under* the elements consecrated and received, Calvin contended that Christ, in all the fullness of his risen being, was in heaven, and his presence was a *spiritual* reality. In his comprehension of this historical debate, Nevin states that in

3. Ibid.
4. Ibid., 50.
5. Ibid., 41.
6. Ibid., 45.
7. Nevin, *Mystical Presence*, 84.

the Reformed Church the participation of the communicant with Christ's flesh and blood was fundamentally spiritual, with the concept of localized presence entirely dismissed.[8] Even so, while the bread and wine "cannot be said to comprehend or include the body of the Saviour in any sense," Calvin retained the language of real presence, but only "as synonymous with *true* presence; by which he means a presence that brings Christ truly into communion with the believer in his human nature, as well as in his divine nature."[9] This is far more than mere theological hairsplitting or semantics; Nevin is advancing and advocating an understanding of this vexing issue of *real presence* with conceptual language that attempts to mediate conflicting positions held on several sides, manifesting a catholicity that exceeds the confines of obdurate confessionalism.

Nevin also embraces Calvin's understanding of the role of the Holy Spirit in the Eucharist. Holding to the conviction that Christ's body (read: *fullness of being*) remains in heaven, and though the communicant believer is bound to this earth, "by the power of the Holy Ghost . . . the obstacle of such vast local distance is fully overcome, so that in the sacramental act, while the outward symbols are received in an outward way, the very body and blood of Christ are at the same time inwardly and supernaturally communicated to the worthy receiver, for the real nourishment of his new life."[10] The perspicacity of Nevin's premise is evident in the expressed conviction that the Eucharist offers more than the other theorems on *real presence* have demonstrated the capacity to convey: ". . . in the Holy Supper . . . Christ communicates *himself* to his Church; not simply a right to the grace that resides in his person, or an interest by outward grant in the benefits of his life and death; but his person itself, as the ground and fountain, from which these other blessings may be expected to flow . . . Christ first, and *then* his benefits."[11]

All, of course, is dependent upon *faith*. However, Nevin will not allow faith to determine the innate quality of the sacrament as defined within his system and explication. Here, too, Nevin's position resonates with that of John Calvin, where faith becomes the vehicle of both perception and receptivity (also and always as a gift of God): "Christ communicates himself to us, in the real way now mentioned, *under the form* of the sacramental

8. Ibid., 55.
9. Ibid., 56.
10. Ibid.
11. Ibid., 116.

mystery as such. . . . All is by the same Spirit; and for the communicant himself, all hangs upon the condition of faith."[12] Dr. Gordan Lathrop, in his book *Holy Things: A Liturgical Theology*, states that "to take up the holy things and to be holy people, ought to be the continual theme of any helpful liturgical theology."[13] Perhaps, then, Lathrop—a Lutheran liturgical scholar who, ironically, makes no reference to Nevin's work—would appreciate Nevin's observation when he writes that we believers "need holiness as well as pardon"[14]—a holiness that is not based or dependent upon the individual effort, but is rather a consequence of remaining, in faith, open "to receive continuously the stream of life that flows upon him from Christ."[15]

It is perhaps Nevin's use of the term *mystical* that has created or could present the greatest obstacle to wider appreciation for and acceptance of his sacramental proposal. It is ironically the same term which, in Nevin's intended usage, promises a more enthusiastic response among some participants in ecumenics. Richard Wentz provides a helpful opening to a more sympathetic perspective on Nevin's employment of *mystical* when he argues that for Nevin "the life and work of Jesus Christ is a participation in the life of the world that affects a new birth in which we all may share. There is a union, incorporation into Christ that also forms the life of Christ in the human."[16] Our thinking is then shaped by the *mystical* union of Christ with humanity, while the incarnation, understood to be Christ's *mystical* union with the world, elevates both our thinking and the world beyond the natural order.[17] Nevin comes close to offering his own definition of the term *mystical* in describing the sacramental transaction of the Eucharist as "a *mystery*; nay, in some sense an actual *miracle*. The Spirit works here in a way that transcends, not only the human understanding, but the ordinary course of the world also in every other view."[18]

Interestingly, Lutheran theologian Gordan Lathrop sounds a note that resonates with Nevin's sacramental incarnationalism when he writes, "Christians believe that Jesus Christ is present in . . . the meal of the assembly. Because he is present, the assembly is fully the catholic church. Because

12. Nevin, *Mystical Presence*, 171.

13. Lathrop, *Holy Things*, 11.

14. Nevin, *Mystical Presence*, 180.

15. Ibid., 221.

16. Wentz, *John Williamson Nevin*, 22.

17. Ibid., 45–46.

18. Nevin, *Mystical Presence*, 112.

he is present, this assembly says all that Christians have to say about the ordering of things."[19] Nevin himself frames an analogous observation regarding the universal significance of the incarnation of Christ when he affirms it to be "the scope of all God's counsel and dispensations in the world. The mystery of the universe is interpreted in the person of Jesus Christ."[20] Nevin's use of *mystical*—in describing union with Christ—while sacramental and incarnational, "is not merely moral, or unintentional . . . but is rather substantial, real." As Nevin states the case: "As joined to Christ, then, we are *one* with him in his life. . . . Christ communicates his own life substantially to the soul on which he acts, causing it to grow into his very nature. This is the *mystical union*; the basis of our whole salvation."[21]

In the contemporary culture where much of the religious fervor smacks not only of individualism and subjectivism, but also displays a tendency toward a modern form of gnostic dualism, Nevin offers an important and critical corrective. Given Wentz's proposal that Nevin wishes to reconcile the inward and outward dimensions of the Eucharist (as traditionally understood), it is reasonable to anticipate that he would contend against any form of dualism, gnostic or otherwise. Nowhere is this more evident than in Nevin's admirable discussion of the incarnation, where he provides a holistic perspective on human nature:

> Body and soul are alike essential to the conception of true human life; and if Christ's life be in us at all in a real way, it seems impossible to avoid the conclusion that it must be in us, as such human life, in the one form of existence as truly and fully as in the other. Both forms of existence constitute in fact but the same living nature; and the extension of this nature, by the power of the Spirit, to the soul of the believer, involves necessarily the reproduction of the life as a whole in his person.[22]

Throughout this work Nevin emphasizes the "relational quality of all aspects of human existence."[23] This relational aspect of Nevin's thought is clearly discernible when he asserts that we "are brought to God, not by doctrine or example, but only by being made to participate in the divine nature itself; and this participation is made possible to us only through the

19. Lathrop, *Holy Things*, 208.

20. Nevin, *Mystical Presence*, 192.

21. Ibid., 159.

22. Ibid., 186.

23. Quoted in Wentz, *John Williamson Nevin*, 44.

person of Christ; who is therefore the very substance of our salvation."[24] But again, this relational feature, this participatory encounter in which Christ is communicated, must be understood holistically, so that should such communication "be *real* at all, as distinguished from figurative, imputative, or simply moral, it must be real for the whole [person], not simply for a part of the [person]."[25] Those who would question the contemporary relevance of Nevin's focus here would be encouraged to attend a "Lord's Supper" in any number of *new paradigm* Christian communities, where the corruption of the sacrament is matched only by the parody of a gnostic-like mystery cult ritual!

Among the contributions Nevin makes to the ecumenical movement is his description of that which makes Christianity unique among the pluralities of contemporary religions. The ecumenical movement has already begun dialogue beyond the boundaries of confessional Christian communities, seeking to engage in a more pluralistic round-table discussion. Without sounding a harsh tone of *triumphalism*, Nevin states with full and genuine conviction that "Christianity . . . is a *life*. Not a rule or mode of life simply; not something that in its own nature requires to be reduced to practice; for that is the character of all morality, but life in its very nature and constitution, and as such the actual substance of truth itself. This is its grand distinction. Here it is broadly separated from all other forms of religion that ever have claimed, or ever can claim, the attention of the world."[26] Stated in even more forceful language, Christianity represents far more than the conceptual category of one religious system of belief and practice competing with others, but is rather *ontologically* unique: "As then the whole human race, naturally considered, lay organically in *Adam*, and all history is thus but the development of what was in his nature included; so *Christ* also is the real bearer of the entire Church, the new creation, the sanctified humanity, as he not only by virtue of his atonement destroys the old, but to the same extent creates the new also, and forms his own sacred image in every believing soul."[27]

When Nevin turns his attention to the confessional documents of the Reformed faith that are offered in support of his thesis, it is not surprising to discover a particular respect and affection for the Heidelberg Catechism

24. Ibid., 202.
25. Ibid., 174.
26. Ibid., 201.
27. Ibid., 221.

(itself intended to be an ecumenical effort relevant to its own historical context). Question and answer number 76 of the Catechism offer a striking example of the support this particular document gives to Nevin's argument throughout; in particular, the second part of the answer, which reads: "Through the Holy Spirit, who lives both in Christ and in us, we are united more and more to Christ's blessed body. And so, although he is in heaven and we are on earth, we are flesh of his flesh and bone of his bone. And we forever live on and are governed by one Spirit, as the members of our body are by one soul."[28]

Hints, then, of Nevin's having been influenced by the catholic teaching of the Catechism can be found throughout *The Mystical Presence*, particularly in the following quotations, provided in detail so as to convey the compelling quality of Nevin's theological and sacramental conviction:

> As the mystical union embraces the whole Christ, so we too are embraced by it not in a partial but *whole* way. . . . A new life . . . to become truly ours, must extend to us in the totality of our nature. It must fill the understanding, and rule the will, enthrone itself in the soul and extend itself out over the entire body. . . . The mystery now affirmed is accomplished, not in the way of two different forms of action, but by one and the same single and undivided process. . . . Soul and body, in their ground, are but one life; identical in their origin; bound together by mutual interpenetration subsequently at every point; and holding forever in the presence and power of the self-same organic law.[29]

Richard Wentz offers yet another reason for Nevin's appreciative use of the Heidelberg Catechism. Wentz contends that for Nevin the Catechism "becomes a model for systematic theology by organizing the symbolic content of the faith and passing it on without being caught up in party spirit. It does not represent abstract reflection, compiling a scheme or theory of the Christian faith for others to examine. 'The Catechism is more than mere doctrine. It is doctrine apprehended and represented continually in the form of life.'"[30] It is in the *symbolic* character that genuine authority is to be found. Not simply because the Catechism has been shaped by the religious life of the Church, but rather because any *symbol* owes its existence to having been apprehended in life. "That is why the catechism is organized in

28. Christian Reformed Church, *Ecumenical Creeds and Reformed Confessions*, 46.

29. Nevin, *Mystical Presence*, 161.

30. Wentz, *John Williamson Nevin*, 39.

such a way that it represents the story of human existence itself."[31] One need only consider the content of the three sections of the Catechism to authenticate the point Wentz has made; one could say that the life of the Catechism is representative of the way in which it captures, holds, and conveys the drama of human existence and the whole history of salvation.

The ecumenical implications of Nevin's important contribution to a sacramental theology could be enumerated in a linear form. For example, the list of articles—numbering 1 through 24—with which Nevin summarizes his argument provides a vehicle by which exploration could be made of their implicit value in contributing to *shared communion* or even *organic union*. Or, one could highlight select formulae in *The Mystical Presence*, and suggest ways in which each one chosen might further ecumenical dialogue. For instance, in his analysis of Nevin's use of *mystical*, Wentz drops the following clue: "Here is an idea that approaches the concept of theosis and deification so central to Eastern Christianity."[32] By far the greatest promise to be discovered in Nevin's work, and an achievement of unqualified ecumenical import, is in his attention to the intrinsic association of incarnational, christological, sacramental, and ecclesiological foci, and the *symbols* representing each and all together. Even such comments as the following demonstrate Nevin's continuing relevance to contemporary ecumenical and theological debate: "The persons of the adorable Trinity are indeed distinct. But we must beware of sundering them into abstract subsistences, one without the other. They subsist in the way of the most perfect mutual inbeing and intercommunication."[33]

Of equal importance to the ecumenical endeavor, and again an area to which Nevin's thought could make an invaluable contribution, is an assessment of the role of what have been generally referred to as "new paradigm" or "mega" churches. While at first blush the following critical observation seems to discredit and exclude any of these communities from ecumenical engagement, Nevin's critique could also be appreciated as an outline of the fundamental issues needing to be addressed. In this more favorable perspective—and even though Nevin's target is other than "new paradigm" communities of faith—his critical assessment could provide the parameters for initial engagement and eventual dialogue:

31. Ibid.
32. Ibid., 22.
33. Nevin, *Mystical Presence*, 212.

> Both [rationalism and pietism] are antagonistic to the idea of the
> Church. . . . Both make the *objective* to be nothing, and the *subjec-*
> *tive* to be all in all. Both undervalue the *outward*, in favor of what
> they conceive to be the *inward*. . . . Both, of course, sink the *sacra-*
> *ments* to the character of mere outward rituals, or possibly deny
> their necessity altogether. Both affect to make much of the *bible*,
> at least in the beginning; though sometimes indeed it is made to
> yield . . . to the imagination of some superior inward light more
> directly from God; and in all cases, it is forced to submit to the
> tyranny of mere private interpretation, as the only proper measure
> of its sense.[34]

Because all healthy and constructive judgments begin with one's own household, it could be that we "mainline/old-line" Christian communities should first assess *our own* practices by the standards implied in Nevin's critique before approaching—or what is worse, *reproaching*—those who worship in any one "new paradigm" setting of the church. In any case, Nevin's critical observation calls each of us back to a healthy accountability, with acknowledgment, confession, repentance, and renewal, and to a more faithful engagement with the Christ of the eucharistic-evangel as a worthy objective, regardless of our communal or confessional affiliation.

The points at which Nevin's complete work in *The Mystical Presence* contributes to my proposal could extend well beyond the current chapter, perhaps constituting a separate book altogether. However, in fulfillment of the second goal of the chapter stated as one of two objectives, I will cover some of the more salient points of Nevin's work that promise to yield insightful and useful designs for my proposal.

One such point is raised in reference to an observation made by Reinhold Niebuhr in *The Living Theological Heritage of the United Church of Christ*, where Niebuhr writes that "holding discussions about the possibility of union, or even raising the question of whether such discussions should be held, invariably raises the questions of identity and self-understanding."[35] Implicitly Nevin's treatise advances the argument for a Christian identity that is shaped not so much by doctrine as by a life and a living relationship, and that this dynamic is most evident in the event of the eucharistic-evangel. Moreover, his desire to harmonize the inward and the outward dimensions of the Eucharist, advocating an intrinsic bond between the two dimensions of religious life as well, presses home the need to formulate a

---

34. Ibid., 140.

35. Hilkke, *Living Theological Heritage*, 460.

definition of a genuine Christian identity that is (trans)formed and maintained from within a relational context—even though that context be restricted to a liturgical setting.

Nevin's project also supports an understanding of the development of a Christian identity that is more of a process than is often implied in conversional models and more ecumenical than it is parochial, since the focus is on the singular sacramental event of the whole Christian Church. His thesis allows for degrees of maturation in self-understanding and in cultivating thinking that is conformed to the "mind of Christ." At the same time, Nevin recognizes the limitations imposed upon our growth in Christ, as each Christian "carries in [him or herself] two forms of existence, a law of 'sin and death' on the one hand, and 'the law of the spirit of life in Christ' on the other; as the power of the last is continually opposed and restrained by the power of the first."[36] Such an honest appraisal prevents my proposal for the promotion of a distinctive identity formation from the tendency to seek any form of perfected identity, either in its foundational rationale or stated objectives. Nevertheless, Nevin's proposal vindicates my own as the expressed interest in promoting a concept of a distinctive Christian identity that pushes beyond all doctrinal and/or confessional convictions, one grounded more in the commendation of a deepening relationship with the living Christ—in and through the eucharistic-evangel as a liturgical event shared by almost all Christian communities—who must always be at the center of a catholic, ecumenical identity.

In the conclusion to his book, Wentz offers a comment that describes in general terms what could also be considered further validation for my contention that Nevin's work supports the concept of a distinctive Christian identity exceeding the boundary markers of confessional and/or denominational configurations:

> Nevin develops the notion of catholicity as wholeness in response to the American inclination to think of catholicity as allness . . . the mystical union of the divine and human . . . is a worldly and dynamic proceeding . . . the Incarnation represents a radical and realized catholicity. It is realized because it is present in the world, radical insofar as it rejects all realized claims to the fullness of the truth of God other than in Christ . . . catholicity required a movement beyond individualistic salvation, into a vocational concern

36. Nevin, *Mystical Presence*, 166.

for the shaping of civilization . . . the community of faith . . . represents the presence of a new creation in the midst of the old.[37]

In an age when the ecumenical endeavor seems to have stalled or has experienced an impasse, the work of Nevin provides suggestive ideas for reenergizing those same dialogues, perhaps even to the point of providing the means to move past current obstacles into a more fruitful exchange of ecumenical ideas. My interest in Nevin is in the way his theological reflections on the Eucharist, even while attempting to reclaim a more faithful position congruent with the Reformed tradition, offers a more expansive horizon for discussing those concepts endemic to the sacrament that have frustrated and at times paralyzed ongoing conversation and the attempt to expand *shared communion* as a manifestation of greater visible unity in Christ. I find great promise in Nevin's promotion of the "relational" concept of *real presence* and in his attempt to move beyond the focus on localization (i.e., in the elements themselves); and Nevin's concept of the "mystical union" *could* be the basis for furthering conversations with our brothers and sisters in the Eastern Church.

On the whole, the Mercersburg theology has historically demonstrated a deep and abiding appreciation for the wealth of insight and inspiration available to the individual Christian and the Church in the "Great Tradition." A reclamation of the beauty of the eucharistic-evangel and the accompanying appreciation of the way in which this singular sacramental event enriches and enlarges our relationship with Christ—individually and corporately as well—is founded on the belief that the resources for such "reclamation" are already in storage in the "Great Tradition" of our faith. John Williamson Nevin and his colleagues, past and present, are testimony to the value of such exploration and exposition.

---

37. Wentz, *John Williamson Nevin*, 144–47.

SEVEN

The Transformational Process
and Summation

… the Holy Spirit fuses us with Christ by His divine fire, not only morally, but
naturaliter, as the Fathers express it, that is, physically, so that we form one
body with Him. So also, operating on the same principle, He brings about within
our interior not only a moral conversion, or a new juridical relation to God, but
an altogether real, physical assimilation and union with God. By the reception of
grace our soul takes a higher nature; that is, with regard to its interior condition,
its faculties, and its activity it is transformed into the image of the divine nature,
is raised to an incomparably higher life, and according to the teaching of the
Fathers is, in a certain true and exalted sense, divinized.[1]

The Transformational Process

THROUGHOUT THIS ESSAY I have made use of the term *transformation*
(and the associated term *process*) without having offered a concise
definition. I have done so in order to allow for an open-ended interpretation of the term; that is, theologically the term could refer to such traditional categories as *sanctification*, maturation in faith, faith development,
or growing into/conforming to the *image of Christ*. Both *conversion* and
the biblical *metanoia* are also implicit in my use of the term *transformation*. What I have attempted to stress throughout is that this is a process

1. Scheeben, *Mysteries of Christianity*, 502–3.

and is dependent upon the variables of both faith and the influence of God's Holy Spirit; nevertheless, the process itself is grounded in a regular (I would argue weekly!) engagement with the *real presence* of Christ in the eucharistic-evangel.

However, my employment of *transformation* has been under the rubric of the *transformational process* as defined and described by Dr. James E. Loder of Princeton Theological Seminary in his inaugural address delivered in 1979.[2] Though his focus is on the dynamics evident in Christian education, the steps in this transformational process as described by Dr. Loder are certainly relevant to my proposal.

Dr. Loder indicates five steps in the transformational process: 1) Conflict borne of persistence; 2) interlude and scanning; 3) insight felt with intuitive force; 4) release and redirection of psychic energy bound up with the original conflict; and 5) interpretation which tests the insight for coherence with the terms of the conflict and for correspondence with the public context of the original conflict.[3] When these steps are applied to the narrative of Luke 24 (i.e., the Emmaus road event), the correlation between Dr. Loder's schema and the story from Luke's Gospel would take shape in the following way: 1) Conflict borne of persistence (Luke 24:13–24); 2) interpretation and scanning (Luke 24:25–29); 3) insight felt with intuitive force (Luke 24: 30–31); 4) release and redirection of psychic energy bound up with the original conflict (Luke 24:32); and 5) interpretation which tests the original insight for coherence with the public context of the original conflict (Luke 24:33–35). Having suggested that the Lucan text is paradigmatic of early Christian liturgy and so represents that distinctive form of Christian worship as the essential unity of *Word* and *Sacrament*, the above model (Loder's steps) of correlation discloses the movement of the transformational process within the context of this liturgical form.

Furthermore, the interests of Dr. Loder in relating the transformational process to Christian education bear decisively on my proposal, in that I would argue there should be no disconnect between the content and format of the ongoing educational ministry of the Church and the structure and content of the Lord's Day worship event.[4] Although I have argued

2. Loder, "Transformation in Christian Education."

3. Ibid., 6.

4. One of the ways in which this same issue has been addressed in sections of the Reformed heritage (and in particular with those churches associated with the Mercersburg theology) is by use of the Heidelberg Catechism throughout the year as instrumental to the preaching ministry in the context of worship. I am suggesting that there be a similar

throughout this essay that the liturgy of *Word* and *Sacrament* is that essential form of a distinctive Christian liturgical practice, having a central role in the transformation and maintenance of a distinctive Christian identity, I would also and at the same time advocate the importance or centrality of Christian education in strengthening the entire *process*.

I would propose that the program of Christian education in the life of the local congregation become that medium of learning, insight, and inspiration that endeavors to bring the biblical, theological, and liturgical traditions of the Church catholic to bear on the identity formation of the Christian disciple. The educational program of the congregation, together with the regular celebration of the liturgy of *Word* and *Sacrament*, will enhance the transformational process, maintaining and strengthening a distinctive Christian identity, eventuating in a distinctive form of Christian ministry and mission beyond the four walls of the local church. There is sufficient "meat" in the aspects of the contemporary Christian's confrontation with a culture becoming increasingly secularized and materialistic to warrant the contention that each of the steps of Loder's model are evident week to week in the persistent conflict between what it means to *be* "Christian" in a world that ranges from hostile to indifferent.

Therefore I would further advocate the following parallels with Loder's five steps in the transformational process:

1. Conflict borne with persistence = the persistent conflict evident in the formation of Christian identity, including such theological categories as *simul justus et peccator* and the "already-not yet" eschatological dimension to Christian existence;

2. interlude and scanning = the enduring interaction between the biblical and theological traditions and the transformation and maintenance of a distinctive Christian identity implicit in the educational process;

3. insight felt with intuitive force = the encounter with the *real presence* in/through the liturgy of *Word* and *Sacrament*;

4. release and redirection of psychic energy bound up with the original conflict = weekly *acknowledgment, recognition, and confession* of the full (true!) identity of Jesus Christ as the One who *fulfills* the Scriptures (*spoken Word*) and whose distinctive identity is disclosed as the *crucified-risen-reigning-and-returning* One (*visible Word*), and the

and intentional connection facilitated between the ministry of education in the church and the event of Lord's Day worship in the eucharistic-evangel.

receptivity of this encounter as that which fuels the transformation of the believer's personal identity and that of the corporate body as well;

5. interpretation which tests the insight for coherence with the terms of the conflict and for correspondence with the public context of the original conflict = the outward and ongoing expression of the transformational process as ministry and mission, both within the community of faith and well beyond her own boundaries; knowing the true identity of Jesus Christ facilitates the capacity to enter the world, not in a confrontational manner, but with every intent to communicate the fullness of his love, mercy, grace, forgiveness, and reconciling presence with others who are yet estranged and lost in the labyrinth of lies pronounced and sponsored by a "culture of death."

Thus the goal of transformation calls for an integrated relationship between the educational, liturgical, ministerial, and missional life of the Christian community. While my primary concern has been to focus on the liturgical practices of the Church, here I begin to advocate the relationship between liturgy and those other aspects of Christian existence that, together, enhance the entire transformational process.

Summation

Word and *Sacrament* not only belong together, but *essentially* belong together; it is the Word of God that takes the water of baptism and the bread and wine of the Eucharist and consecrates them for their sacramental use; and it is the Word of God that points, as witness, to our Lord and gives the elements of the sacraments their gospel form and content. This is the theological principle by which I have advocated the essential union of *Word* and *Sacrament*, which forms the distinctive nature of Christian worship. And it is this particular liturgical configuration that serves to enhance the transformation and maintenance of a distinctive Christian identity. From the vantage point of this particular theological-liturgical principle, I would affirm that when God reveals Godself to us, God does so in such a way that both *form* and *meaning* (i.e., *spoken Word* and *visible Word* in fluid relationship) conjoin; the signs of the sacrament need the "proclaimed Word" to disclose their deepest—their *holistic*—meaning!

The transformation that then ensues from this liturgical event is not merely the "changed or 'strangely warmed' heart" of a person; rather this form of transformation creates a whole new person (in Christ, with Christ, for Christ and the world—to the glory of God!) as well as a new *Weltan-shauung* for both individual and community. From this perspective such transformation can truly be said to bear an *eschatological* character. And I can only offer my fervent prayer that the position and proposal advocated throughout this essay will prove useful in the ongoing endeavor to better comprehend the essential relationship between the liturgy, the sacraments, and the transformation and maintenance of a distinctive Christian identity. I close this chapter with the profound words of the liturgical prayer:

> Grant to your servants that they may keep in their lives to the baptism they have received in faith.
>
> Grant that the sacraments we have received at Easter may continue to live in our minds and hearts.
>
> Grant that we may initiate and achieve what we celebrate and profess.
>
> Grant that we who have celebrated the Easter ceremonies may hold to them in life and conduct.[5]

5. Wainwright, *Doxology*, 423.

EIGHT

Final Comments
and Personal Observations

As we continue into the twenty-first century, those of us in the Stone-Campbell
heritage need to place less emphasis on judging who is "saved" and who is not
"saved," and spend more time lifting up Jesus Christ. It is not my job to make
everyone believe what I believe about baptism, the Lord's Supper, the Holy Spirit,
etc. But it is my job to love them as Jesus loves them and to lift him up
so that he will draw all people to himself.[1]

SOME WILL NO DOUBT find the above expression to be hopelessly naïve,
or at the very least, overly pietistic and terribly sentimental; but I am
stimulated by this comment of Rick Grover's both for his candor and for
the way in which it embodies the essence of what I have proposed throughout this essay. Although not his intent, from my vantage point, even the
Roman Catholic could embrace the concept of "lifting up Jesus Christ" as
reminiscent of the elevation of the host during the Mass, a visible reminder
of the need to elevate Christ above all else, and to that degree alone a form
of *rapprochement*! More importantly, Grover's comment underscores the
necessity to ever keep in focus the purpose for which we enter into ecumenical engagements; if it is not to expand the "visibility" of Christ in this
world, then one could rightly demand to know the purpose of advancing
greater "visible" unity.

1. Carson, Foster, and Holloway, *One Church*, 55.

Furthermore, Grover captures the essential nature of what I have asserted throughout this essay to be the soul of a distinctive Christian identity—"to love [all people] as Jesus loves them and to lift [Christ] up so that he will draw all people to himself." Should the Eucharist be perceived as little more than a liturgical form, even the highest of liturgical forms, and not that event (i.e., the eucharistic-evangel!) in and through which Christ seeks to transform, mold, and shape the Christian character and identity of his people, then I fail to see why this particular worshipful practice has held such a central place in the vastness of liturgical expressions throughout the Church catholic. Grover's comment resonates with my contention that the central power and purpose of this worshipful event—beyond all associations noted in the history of liturgical theology—is to create and sustain a people who enter the world prepared to "lift [Christ] up so that he will draw all people to himself."

I have argued that a distinctive Christian identity is the product of a transformation through baptism, confirmation, and the persistent practice of the eucharistic-evangel. Unlike baptism and confirmation, the eucharistic-evangel represents the ongoing transformative event and environment; it is the context of a gradual, deliberate, processive, and progressive molding of a distinctive Christian identity (see Eph 4:15–16; Phil 2:5ff.; Col 1:27ff.). The open-telling of God's redemptive history infuses the history and identity of the individual and community with a deep and lasting meaning (read: "eternal life" actualized in the present and anticipatory of future fulfillment!). It is not that we imaginatively "remember" the exodus event, as though we could feel the sand between our toes and hear the roar of the waters parting; it is not that we experience being present at Golgotha, shedding tears of remorse and sorrow, or that we join the women in attending to the tomb of Jesus on that first Easter morning, or even that we travel that dusty road from Jerusalem to Emmaus.

Rather, the conscious and forceful open-telling (as proclamation and *spoken Word*) of the redemptive history of God and his Christ, under the power of the Holy Spirit, discloses his presence with/for us, just as he was with/for these others. It is the *anamnesis* of his redemptive and healing presence that effects the transformation of personal and temporal identity. The sacramental action (*visible Word*) discloses the distinctive nature—the true identity—of Jesus Messiah as the crucified Christ and suffering servant, risen from the dead, ascended to the "right hand of God," and returning in glory, which transforms and maintains a distinctive Christian identity.

So it is that I contend that the eucharistic-evangel is a sacramental encounter with the triune God of love, whose center is Jesus Messiah—as the fulfillment of redemptive history in both *Word* and *Action*, and as the proleptic assurance of the final event of God's coming kingdom (stated with such clarity in 1 Cor 11:26: "For as often as you eat this bread and drink the cup, you proclaim the Lord's death until He comes"). It is the gracious gift of the Father, in communion with the Son, in and through which the healing, reconciling, and transformative power of the Holy Spirit is actualized as a sacramental reality in the life of both the individual believer and the community at large. The panorama of redemptive history (proclaimed) together with the sacramental order (enacted) discloses the divine love of the triune God extended in, to, and for the world—creation and creature, individual and community, past, present, and future:

> The eucharist is the great sacrifice of praise by which the Church speaks on behalf of the whole creation. For the world which God has reconciled is present at every eucharist: in the bread, wine, in the persons of the faithful, and in the prayers they offer for themselves and all people. Christ unites the faithful with himself and includes their prayers within his own intercession so that the faithful are *transfigured* and their prayers accepted. This sacrifice of praise is possible only through Christ, *with* him and *in* him. The bread and wine, fruits of the earth and of human labor, are presented to the Father in faith and thanksgiving. The eucharist signifies what the world is to become: an offering and hymn of praise to the Creator, a universal communion in the body of Christ, a kingdom of justice, love and peace in the Holy Spirit.[2]

The *anamnesis* of the eucharistic-evangel heals the breaches and fragmentations of the temporal and personal dimensions to existence, and is the greatest promise for the furtherance of "visible" unity among the separated brethren. This is the celebration that extends an invitation to the whole of humankind to experience the *anamnesis* and thus to be transformed. It is the *anamnesis* that reveals the *real presence* of Christ to and for the world: "The very celebration of the eucharist is an instance of the Church's participation in God's mission to the world. This participation takes everyday form in the proclamation of the Gospel, service to the neighbor, and faithful presence in the world."[3]

---

2. World Council of Churches, *Baptism, Eucharist, and Ministry*, 10.
3. Ibid., 15.

We may not be able to ascertain (with any certainty) that our *Sitz im Leben* is similar to that of the nascent Christian community. But technological and scientific advances have, in no way, lessened the crisis of Christian identity and mission. There is one experience that remains the same: like those first-century Christians and immediate followers of Jesus, we contemporary disciples continue to struggle with the questions surrounding the proper identification of our Master and of our own identity in relation to him. There are far too many in the contemporary Christian community who, like those first disciples, are influenced by a narrow and limiting christological understanding (i.e., "messianic expectation"). In turn, this has tended to truncate Christian identity, for example, Christians whose identity conforms to the moral teachings of Christ, or those conformed to the character of Christ as "liberator, revolutionary, and social reformer," or those who lay claim to the piety of Christ; and this is not to mention the way in which denominational and confessional identity markers have had a greater influence on the identity of Christians than has the crucified-risen-reigning-returning Christ in the fullness of his identity and Lordship!

The eucharistic-evangel will, I contend, not only confront such limited expectations and interpretations, but will transform and enlarge them well beyond the restrictive boundaries mentioned in the above paragraph. For here, in the liturgy of *Word* and *Sacrament*, we as individuals and as a community are—like our first-century counterparts—encountered by the one who embodies all the richness and vitality of redemptive history, while at the same time adding that distinctive dimension to his own personal identity (i.e., as the crucified-risen-reigning-returning one), which remains for many a "stumbling bock . . . and folly." Nonetheless, it is this one who confronts us, as individual Christians and as Church, in and through this most central, critical, and crucial liturgical event; seeking to do with us that which he accomplished with those first-century disciples, seeking the transformation and maintenance of a distinctive Christian identity among those he would send forth into the world to serve in both ministry and mission.

The encounter with our crucified and risen Lord assures the transformation of identity, and it is this essential reality of the liturgy of *Word* and *Sacrament* that mandates weekly celebration; the essential unity of distinctive Christian liturgy, distinctive Christian identity, and distinctive ministry and mission contribute to the ecumenical characteristics of the event and serve to promote discussions concerning the relationship between liturgy, identity, mission, and the endeavor to further visible unity. I state this as essential because

> when Christians' missionary and social vision is separated from their sacramental life, both the sacraments and Christian witness are made trivial and the transcendence of the Gospel is lost. For example, if mission becomes only goodwill responses to human problems, or if evangelism becomes only proclaiming to save individual souls, our progress in witness and service will come to nought. Such mission becomes solidarity with others without the presence of Christ. The brokenness of the world—symbolized by racism, the threat of nuclear holocaust, the denial of human rights—is more than social problems. Fundamentally, this brokenness is a denial of the sacramental character of life given by God, and only a sacramental community will know the difference. Conversely, if the sacraments become merely institutional rites or rituals of personal piety without the conviction that they are empowerments for God's mission in the world, then baptism, eucharist, and ministry are distorted. We become a church without any expectation of the Kingdom of God. But for the community which awaits the Kingdom, which knows it is called to be the stigmata, the marks of suffering, in its own life and members, the sacraments are the signs of God's solidarity with the poor, the suffering, and rejected of the world.[4]

Throughout this essay my desire has been to detail the ethical dimensions of the process of transformation through the concerted effort to disclose the relationship between liturgy, identity, and mission; as such my position merely serves to strengthen the ties between the individual, the community of faith, and the world in both worship and ethical practice, that is, *praxis*. This relationship between individual and community is indispensable to the eucharistic-evangel: "Therefore, in eucharistic communion we receive Christ, Christ himself; and our union with him, which is a gift and grace for each individual, brings it about that in him we are also associated in the unity of his body which is the church."[5] However, "this is not to imply that, through the Eucharist, God bestows grace wholesale on the entire group. If individuals benefit . . . it is specifically as Christians whose vocation binds them up with a larger family which is part of their call."[6]

4. Crow, "BEM: Challenge and Promise," 486.

5. Bernier, *Bread Broken and Shared*, 92.

6. Ibid., 97.

Transformation should not be perceived as merely a private affair; rather transformation serves to strengthen the reality of our being conformed to the image of Christ, bound to the Body of Christ, and sent forth to serve the world in the name of Christ—a reality conceived in baptism, nurtured further in confirmation, and renewed in the weekly celebration of *Word* and *Sacrament*.

Such transformation thus places the identity of the individual squarely within the identity of the community broadly defined as the Body of Christ. St. Augustine alluded to such an understanding of the essential nature of the relationship between individual and community in the eucharistic-evangel when he said: "If you are the Body of Christ and his members, it is your mystery which has been placed on the altar of the Lord; you receive your own mystery. You answer 'Amen' to what you are."[7] It is such an understanding as this that leads one to a deeper appreciation for the relationship between the *real presence* of Christ, the transformation of identity at both individual and corporate levels, and the imperative for weekly celebration of this worshipful event, in the desire to strengthen and maintain a distinctive Christian identity:

> The quote from St. Augustine serves to remind us that there is a "more and less" aspect of our being part of the Body of Christ. We know that the struggle to "put on Christ," as St. Paul says, is a lifelong one; it is never-ending. Precisely here does the eucharistic presence of Christ urge us on, challenging us to respond more fully to the mystery which is ours. If our faith is weak, and the quality of our lives barely Christ-like, Jesus' presence within will not be very obvious. On the other hand, as we grow into the likeness of Christ and bring to the Eucharist a faith-filled presence, the eucharistic Christ will more and more become enfleshed within us. We will be saying "Amen" to the reality which is visible for all to see; we will become more fully in Christ.[8]

This definition of the eucharistic-evangel, which brings the individual and community into closer harmony, advocating a transformation of identity that incorporates both levels in the "image of Christ," implies that mission (also in the "image of Christ") must also be achieved harmoniously: "Instead of a Eucharist which seems more a ritual celebration of a group with no real message for or commitment to the world in which we live, it

---

7. Ibid., 122.

8. Bernier, *Bread Broken and Shared*, 123.

becomes a bold proclamation of that same community's concern for others. Our memorial of Christ's sacrifice is something into which we have entered personally; we have made his *words* and *actions* our own."[9]

It should be evident to the reader by now that one reason for having stressed transformation of identity as essential or central to this liturgical event is to mitigate the tendency to perceive the liturgy as an isolated ministry—one divorced from the concrete realities of the world in which the Christian is called to serve:

> Perhaps one of the main reasons why so many Christians are left cold by the Eucharist is that we have succeeded in divorcing Christ's actions from our own. Rather than each eucharistic celebration being an expression and celebration of the community's commitment to live for others and to give of itself for the life of the world, it becomes simply a recalling of Christ's own life apart from any ongoing effect from his body, the church. If the loud proclamation that "This is the cup of my blood which will be shed for you" refers only to Christ, Eucharist becomes essentially an exercise in historical memory.[10]

A far healthier perspective on the eucharistic-evangel would acknowledge that, as an encounter with the *real presence* of Christ, this liturgical event remains essential to the transformation and maintenance of a distinctive Christian identity. It requires the openness and receptivity of faith on the part of individual and community alike; "it necessarily requires a response of the faithful because it is intended to make them instruments of salvation in their full capacity."[11] I close this section of the chapter with an observation that captures the tenor and purpose of my proposal:

> In the final analysis, when we ask how Jesus is going to conquer the distance that separates his glorious state from our own, and how the Eucharist can be a victory of one who is absent to become present in a world which conceals him, we know that we are the one who can facilitate or delay the final victory. The eucharistic presence of Christ is at the heart of the church. But it will be a redeeming presence for us only if the whole mystery of Christ's life is accepted and lived. Only in this way will the church become the presence of Christ in the world.[12]

9. Ibid., 85.
10. Ibid.
11. Ibid., 127.
12. Ibid., 129.

Personal Observations

After thirty years as an ordained pastor, I consider "liturgical theology" important if not central to the task of professional ministry. Having completed this project and proposal, I am convinced that such theological investigation and reflection are essential to pastoral ministry; primarily because it is in the liturgy of the church that one's theological concepts and understanding as "pastoral theologian" are given particular expression. A disciplined study of both the form and content of the liturgy forces one to reconsider all previously held theological convictions and to come to a deeper appreciation for the pastoral applicability of the well-known phrase, *lex orandi, lex credenda.*

To borrow a metaphor from the realm of music, if theological conceptualization is the *lyric,* then liturgy is the *score.* While the lyric in and of itself is meaningful and poetic, it is the score that brings the lyric to rhythmic expression; the same lyric pulses with life as a song to be shared by many voices; the score seems to breathe life into the lyric; both the meaning and poetic nature of the lyric are enhanced from within the score. Liturgy breathes life into theological categories and doctrines of our faith confession; in and through the liturgy we are gifted with a deeper understanding of those same doctrines and confessions of faith that would otherwise remain abstract, if not divorced from life itself.

Liturgical theology at its best is to be perceived as related to every other dimension of the church's life and ministry. Christian life, personal and corporate devotion, ethics, mission and ministry, the educational aspect of the church, theological reflection—all these and more are related to liturgy like spokes to the hub of a wheel. The form, even more the content, of our liturgy will reflect theological convictions and anthropological concerns. The discipline of liturgical theology will challenge us to consider and reconsider what we are all about as a Christian community—what we are and what we are *called* to become. In a strict sense liturgy is "ritual practice"; but in a much broader sense it is a "form of life" involving *praxis* (as the repeated practice of reflection-action-reflection). From whatever direction we approach liturgy, we will soon discover that other areas of the church's life and practice begin to converge in such deliberations.

In this essay I have sought to enlarge the basic affirmation of Karl Barth when he writes (concerning the church's liturgy) that "the primary *content* of the church service corresponds to its primary ground. Whatever takes place in it can be concerned only with the execution of the will and command of the Lord of the church. And His will and command is that the church *exist* and *continue*. The work of the Holy Spirit in the service is to bring this about."[13] The liturgy of *Word* and *Sacrament* is the fullest expression of both this *will* and *command* for the church's existence and continuance. Obsessive attention given to the order of the liturgy will only lead us away from the central thrust of the need to preserve their union as the fullest expression of Christian liturgy.

While the question of *frequency* of celebration can be raised in light of my proposal, I would stress the necessity for observing the "eighth day"—the Lord's Day—the day of resurrection as the essential day for the community to gather at this communal feast. The Lord's Day must remain the occasion for the joyous celebration of the liturgy as the "new day." This is the day on which the assembly gathers for instruction, prayer, celebration, and fellowship, and is therefore the principle day for the liturgy of *Word* and *Sacrament*.

The liturgical practice of the church has undergone extensive change and variation over the long history of the Christian community, and continues to experiences significant changes in both form and content as ever new communities of faith evolve in a variety of settings—cultural and global. The purpose of the present essay has been to provoke thought and conversation concerning the *essential nature* of the Christian liturgy. While it is possible—and perhaps inevitable—that even the eucharistic-evangel (as outlined in this essay) will evolve differently in various settings of the world, I would stand behind my contention that the power of this uniquely Christian event continues to be its capacity to transform and maintain a distinctive Christian identity.

Finally, one cannot read this essay without recognizing the central place given to Christology. I am concerned that my proposal could seem to some to be *christo-monistic*; and yet, my interest throughout has been to highlight the *christo-logical* center of the liturgy. If Christ be considered the "center" of revelation and salvation history (in the sense of both fulfillment and proleptic anticipation), then the unfolding of that same history in the liturgy will bear a *christo-logical* heart and soul![14] I have also argued that

13. Barth, *Knowledge of God and the Service of God according to the Teaching of the Reformation*, 194.

14. Udo Schnelle makes two observations equally relevant to the point I am making. In reference to the appearance stories of the risen Christ, he writes: "Like the resurrection itself, the appearances too are understood as a transcendent event deriving from God,

the liturgy of *Word* and *Sacrament* bears the stamp of the Trinity, and have done so in order to attend to any *christo-monistic* concerns; but there is also and at the same time a definite disclosure of the Triune God in the whole of the eucharistic-evangel, which is inevitable because the whole of salvation history is an event of the Trinity.

Above all, I have attempted throughout this essay to remain faithful to the Scriptures of our faith as they bear decisively on the issue at hand; and so it seems only fitting to give the *last* word, and witness to the one *Word*, to the Scriptures we all as Christians embrace:

> Therefore . . . by the mercies of God, I urge you to present your bodies as a living sacrifice, holy and pleasing to God; this is your spiritual worship. Do not be conformed to this age, but be transformed by the renewing of your mind, so that you may discern what is the good, pleasing, and perfect will of God. (Rom 12:1–2)

---

an event that generated the disciples' transcendent *experiences*. . . . Such experiences of transcendence can be worked through and reconstructed in a twofold manner: 'narratives, in which the experiences of transcendence are made communicable and prepared for retelling, and rituals, whereby such experiences are commemorated and the transcendent reality is evoked.' Both the formula traditions and the narrative traditions do this; in each case they are *necessarily* consolidated in a variety of forms conditioned by their own times and made available for the intersubjective discourse of the churches. Baptism, the Lord's Supper, and worship were ritual locations in which the experiences were renewed and confirmed." Schnelle, *Theology of the New Testament*, 168–69. And in reference to the expansion of christological titles and affirmations (post-resurrection): "Baptism, eucharist, and acclamation stand in an exclusive relation to the name of Jesus; this multiplicity of perspectives points to the new and revolutionary religious experience on which they are based. Alongside theological reflection, the liturgical invocation and ritual worship of Jesus were further anchor points for the construction, development, and expansion of christological ideas." Ibid., 180.

Postscript

THIS ESSAY HAS BEEN directed, primarily, to the academic community, but that is not to say that it should be ignored by the pastor or educated lay person for that matter! As was true of my first book, *United and Uniting*, this essay is fundamentally concerned with offering one model—in this case of the Eucharist—holding potential for furthering ecumenical conversations, and in the most ideal world, opening possibilities for expanding shared communion. If there is novelty in what is offered by my proposal, it is not intentional; as I stated from the outset, I do not find that novelty is, necessarily, the measure of quality in any one theological proposal. Perhaps it was Karl Barth who said it best when he stated—if I am quoting him correctly—that one who enters into the effort of theological explication should always "return to the beginning" or begin at the beginning; which, if correct, implies that we pastoral theologians must always return to the subject at hand, not seeking novelty so much as searching for those origins that have sustained and continue to sustain *ortho-doxy*.

If I can lay claim to anything *unique* in this proposal, it is my interest in moving the dialogue surrounding *real presence* from one of localization to one of transformation as the heart and soul of the eucharistic-evangel. In this manner I also hope to extend the dialogue into those areas that have not been completely neglected, but are seldom the focus of debate, for example, the relationship between the Eucharist and the identity of God's people (individually and as a corporate entity), or the essential uniqueness of *this* sacramental event as a source of empowerment for the Church's ministry and mission, or the necessity for far more frequent—if not weekly—celebration of this sacramental event because it is essential to the development of a distinctive Christian identity in a world saturated with religious pluralism and relativistic convictions—not to mention the increasing measure of both materialism and secularism, here in North America and abroad, or once again the variance in worship across cultural and geographical settings that threatens to introduce novelty at the cost of continuity across the historical horizons of the Church catholic. I offer this essay to the Church at large in the desire to further our dialogue at table regarding the Meal that has been—since the time our Master instituted the same—a hallmark of both Christian worship and identity.

I am aware of the fact that the complexity of the issues surrounding the historical evolution of sacramental theology, and in particular as related to the Eucharist, far exceed the limits of what I have accomplished (or could accomplish!) in an essay of such brevity. Nonetheless, I believe that my proposal has been sufficiently grounded in those dynamics—historical, biblical, theological, and liturgical—to sustain it and to commend it to further dialogue and debate. In this age in which the church—at least in her North American setting—is being challenged on every front, and often for her very existence, giving greater attention to the most central sacrament of the whole of our Christian worship may lead to insights and inspirational dynamics of a profound kind. In point of fact, such serious conversation and dialogue may move us ever closer to ecumenical convergence and a deepened sense of the truth that the vessel in which we sail is One Ship, on One Sea, under the direction of One Captain, and heading to One Port!

Perhaps we can, as Christian brothers and sisters, come to appreciate the fact that our differences in eucharistic perspective are *ours*, but the Meal itself—the eucharistic-evangel—is not *ours* to shape in whatever direction we please, but is the creation and child of the one Christ we all, each of us and all of us together, seek to serve as Lord and Savior, the one who transforms and maintains our distinctive identity as his people—the "Eucharist's Biographer."

Bibliography

Allison, Gregg R. *Historical Theology: An Introduction to Christian Doctrine: A Companion to Wayne Grudem's "Systematic Theology."* Grand Rapids: Zondervan, 2011.

Augustine, Saint. *Confessions.* Translated by R. S. Pine-Coffin. New York: Dorset, 1961.

Balthasar, Hans Urs von. *The Von Balthasar Reader.* Edited by Medard Kehl and Werner Löser. New York: Crossroad, 1982.

Bartels, K. H. "Remember, Remembrance." In *The New International Dictionary of New Testament Theology,* edited by Colin Brown, 3:230–47. Grand Rapids: Zondervan, 1982.

Barth, Karl. *The Knowledge of God and the Service of God according to the Teaching of the Reformation: Recalling the Scottish Confession of 1560.* Translated by J. L. M. Haire and Ian Henderson. New York: Scribner, 1939.

Bernier, Paul. *Bread Broken and Shared: Broadening Our Vision of the Eucharist.* Notre Dame: Ave Maria, 1981.

Braaten, Carl E., and Robert W. Jenson, editors. *Christian Dogmatics.* Vol. 2. Philadelphia: Fortress, 1984.

Brunner, Peter. *Worship in the Name of Jesus.* Translated by M. H. Bertram. St. Louis: Concordia, 1968.

Carson, Glenn Thomas, Douglas A. Foster, and Clinton J. Holloway. *One Church: A Bicentennial Celebration of Thomas Campbell's Declaration and Address.* Abilene, TX: Leafwood, 2008.

Christian Reformed Church. *Ecumenical Creeds and Reformed Confessions.* Grand Rapids: CRC Publications, 1987.

Clifford, Catherine E., editor. *For the Communion of the Churches: The Contribution of the Groupe des Dombes.* Grand Rapids: Eerdmans, 2010.

Crow, Paul A., Jr. "BEM: Challenge and Promise." *Theology Today* 62 (1986) 478–89.

Cullmann, Oscar. *The Christology of the New Testament.* Translated by Shirely C. Guthrie and Charles A. M. Hall. Rev. ed. Philadelphia: Westminster, 1963.

Dillistone, F. W. *Christianity and Symbolism.* London: Collins Clear-Type Press, 1955.

Dyrness, William A., and Veli-Matti Kärkkäinen, editors. *Global Dictionary of Theology.* Downers Grove, IL: InterVarsity, 2008.

Emminghaus, Johannes H. *The Eucharist: Essence, Form, Celebration.* Translated by Matthew J. O'Connell. Collegeville, MN: Liturgical, 1978.

Evangelical and Reformed Church. *The Hymnal.* St. Louis: Eden Publishing House, 1944.

Fackre, Gabriel. "Narrative Theology: An Overview." *Interpretation* 37 (1983) 340–52.

Frei, Hans. *The Identity of Jesus Christ: The Hermeneutical Bases of Dogmatic Theology.* Philadelphia: Fortress, 1975.

Bibliography

Goppelt, Leonhard. *Theology of the New Testament.* Vol. 2, *The Variety and Unity of the Apostolic Witness to Christ.* Translated by John Alsup. Edited by Jürgen Roloff. Grand Rapids: Eerdmans, 1982.

Herbert, A. G. "Memory, Memorial, Remember, Remembrance." In *A Theological Wordbook of the Bible*, edited by Alan Richardson. New York: Macmillan, 1950.

Heron, Alasdair. *Table and Tradition: Towards an Ecumenical Understanding of the Eucharist.* Edinburgh: Handsel, 1983.

Hilke, Elsabeth Slaughter, editor. *The Living Theological Heritage of the United Church of Christ.* Vol. 6, *Growing toward Unity.* Series edited by Barbara Brown Zikmund. Cleveland: Pilgrim, 1998.

Hiltunen, P. Y. "New Religious Movements, Christian." In *Global Dictionary of Theology*, edited by William A. Dyrness and Veli-Matti Kärkkäinen, 603–7. Downers Grove, IL: InterVarsity, 2008.

Hodgson, Peter C. *Jesus—Word and Presence: An Essay in Christology.* Philadelphia: Fortress, 1971.

Hunsinger, George. *The Eucharist and Ecumenism: Let Us Keep the Feast.* New York: Cambridge University Press, 2008.

Jeremias, Joachim. *The Eucharistic Words of Jesus.* Translated by Arnold Ehrhardt. Oxford: Blackwell, 1955.

Johnson, Luke Timothy. *The Gospel of Luke.* Sacra Pagina Series 3. Collegeville, MN: Liturgical, 1991.

Komonchak, Joseph A., Mary Collins, and Dermot A. Lane, editors. *The New Dictionary of Theology.* Wilmington: Michael Glazier, 1987.

Lathrop, Gordon W. *Holy Things: A Liturgical Theology.* Philadelphia: Fortress, 1993.

Leon-Dufour, Xavier. *Dictionary of the New Testament.* Translated by Terrence Prendergast. San Francisco: Harper & Row, 1980.

Loder, James E. "Transformation in Christian Education." Inaugural address, Princeton Theological Seminary, 1979.

Lubac, Henri de. *Corpus Mysticum: The Eucharist and the Church in the Middle Ages.* Translated by Gemma Simmonds. Notre Dame: University of Notre Dame Press, 2007.

McBrien, Richard P. *Catholicism.* Vol. 2. Minneapolis: Winston, 1980.

Mersch, Emile. *The Whole Christ: The Historical Development of the Doctrine of the Mystical Body in Scripture and Tradition.* Translated by John R. Kelly, SJ. London: Dobson, 1938.

Nevin, John W. *The Mystical Presence and Other Writings on the Eucharist.* Edited by Bard Thompson and George H. Bricker. Philadelphia: United Church Press, 1966.

Noll, Mark A. *Jesus Christ and the Life of the Mind.* Grand Rapids: Eerdmans, 2011.

O'Connor, James T. *The Hidden Manna: A Theology of the Eucharist.* 2nd ed. San Francisco: Ignatius, 2005.

Presbyterian Church USA. *Book of Common Worship.* Louisville: Westminster John Knox, 1993.

Rengstorf, K. H. "Jesus Christ." In *The New International Dictionary of New Testament Theology*, edited by Colin Brown, 2:330–43. Grand Rapids: Zondervan, 1982.

Richardson, Alan. *A Theological Word Book of the Bible.* New York: Macmillan, 1951.

Scheeben, Matthias Joseph. *The Mysteries of Christianity.* Translated by Cyril Vollert, SJ. St. Louis: Herder, 1964.

Schillebeeckx, Edward. *Christ, the Sacrament of the Encounter with God.* Kansas City: Sheed, Andrews, & McMeel, 1963.

———. *Interim Report on the Books Jesus & Christ.* New York: Crossroad, 1981.

Schnelle, Udo. *Theology of the New Testament.* Translated by M. Eugene Boring. Grand Rapids: Baker, 2009.

Stoup, George W. *The Promise of Narrative Theology: Recovering the Gospel in the Church.* Atlanta: John Knox, 1981.

Stuhlmueller, Carroll. "The Gospel according to Luke." In *The Jerome Biblical Commentary,* edited by Joseph A. Fitzmyer and Raymond E. Brown, 2:115–64. Englewood Cliffs, NJ: Prentice-Hall, 1968.

Sykes, S. W. "Story and Eucharist." *Interpretation* 37 (1983) 365–76.

Thurian, Max. *The Eucharistic Memorial.* Part 1, *The Old Testament.* Translated by J. G. Davies. Cambridge: Clarke, 2002.

———. *The Eucharistic Memorial.* Part 2, *The New Testament.* Translated by J. G. Davies. Cambridge: Clarke, 2002.

———. *Visible Unity and Tradition.* Translated by W. J. Kerrigan. Baltimore: Helicon, 1962.

Tillich, Paul. *Systematic Theology.* 3 vols. Chicago: University of Chicago Press, 1951–1963.

Torrance, T. F. *Conflict and Agreement in the Church.* 2 vols. London: Lutterworth, 1959.

———. *Theology in Reconciliation.* Grand Rapids: Eerdmans, 1976.

United Church of Christ. *Book of Worship.* Cleveland: Local Church Ministries Worship and Education Ministry Team, 2002.

Vagaggini, Dom Cyprian. *Theological Dimensions of the Liturgy.* Translated by Leonard J. Doyle and W. A. Jurgens. Collegeville, MN: Liturgical, 1976.

Vatican Council II. *The Documents of Vatican II: With Notes and Comments by Catholic, Protestant, and Orthodox Authorities.* Walter M. Abbott, general editor, Joseph Gallagher, translation editor. New York: Guild, 1966.

Volf, Miroslav. *A Public Faith: How Followers of Christ Should Serve the Common Good.* Grand Rapids: Brazos, 2011.

Vondey, Wolfgang. *People of Bread: Redicovering Ecclesiology.* New York: Paulist, 2008.

Wainwright, Geoffrey. *Doxology: The Praise of God in Worship, Doctrine, and Life.* New York: Oxford University Press, 1980.

Walsh, Albert J. D. *United and Uniting: An Ecumenical Ecclesiology for a Church in Crisis.* Eugene, OR: Wipf & Stock, 2011.

Weber, Otto. *Foundations of Dogmatics.* Vol. 2. Translated by Darrell L. Guder. Grand Rapids: Eerdmans, 1983.

Wentz, Richard E. *John Williamson Nevin: American Theologian.* Oxford: Oxford University Press, 1997.

Witherington, Ben III. *The Indelible Image: The Theological and Ethical Thought World of the New Testament.* Vol. 1., *The Individual Witnesses.* Downers Grove, IL: InterVarsity, 2009.

World Council of Churches. *Baptism, Eucharist, and Ministry.* Faith and Order Paper 111. Geneva: WCC, 1982.